The
INNER STUDIO

A DESIGNER'S GUIDE TO
THE RESOURCES OF THE PSYCHE

T0334800

Andrew Levitt

RIVERSIDE ARCHITECTURAL PRESS
University of Waterloo School of Architecture

National Library of Canada Cataloguing in Publication Data

Levitt, Andrew, 1953-2021
The inner studio : a designer's guide to the resources of the pscyhe / Andrew Levitt.

Second edition. | The second edition includes forewords by Anne Bordeleau and Jaliya Fonseka. Includes bibliographical references.
ISBN 978-1-988366-40-1

Canadiana 20220217572
1. Architectural design — Psychological aspects. 2. Design — Psychological aspects. 3. Industrial design — Psychological aspects.

NA2540 .L48 2022   DDC 720.1/9—dc23

EDITOR: Andrea Knight
BOOK DESIGN: Jack Steiner Graphic Design
FRONT COVER AND DIAGRAMS: David Warne
SECOND EDITION PRODUCTION: Bianca Weeko Martin and Philip Beesley
COVER PHOTO: *The House of the Mosaic Atrium, Herculaneum,* by permission Werner Forman Archives

Printed and bound in Canada

07 08 09   3 2 1

For those of you who may not have had the privilege to know Andrew Levitt, to read him or hear him speak, I will try to share here some of the qualities that made him the remarkable and irreplaceable teacher he was. It is difficult to decide what to say about Andrew Levitt in the space of a short preface. Perhaps I can start by sharing how, interested in the 'unseen side of things', Andrew went on to study psychology and worked as a psychotherapist after completing his studies in Architecture at the Architectural Association in London (UK). I can say that he returned to teach architecture, thankfully for us, seeing that, as he writes and I quote, he could "teach design as a process of enriching both the designer and the world". Andrew Levitt authored two key books—*The Inner Studio* (2006) and *Listening to Design* (2018)— each in their own ways opening students to the thoughts of caring for the invisible, for what is not present, caring for emotions, for an idea, caring for others—but also for themselves!

But I could never tell you about Andrew by simply listing his accomplishments, because Andrew was so much more committed to the *how* than he would ever be to the *what*; Andrew always spoke to the full human being—their skills and their soul, their strength and their fears. It is quite stunning to hear former students and colleagues share their appreciation of Andrew. Everyone recognizes this humility, unwavering guidance, the very present presence, and having just the words, advice, reading recommendation for a bad day, for a blank page, for a frustrating drawing, or an apparent impasse.

A list of Andrew's achievements does not tell you much about Andrew, about how he recognized the potential of gaps, the richness of shadows, the importance of moments of pause, the presence of what is not visible and the weight of what lies in darkness. This legacy, slowly and quietly evidenced through decades of teachings in the School of Architecture at the University of Waterloo, is not about what lies on the surface but about profound commitment. It is as much about what he did as it is about what he did not do.

For example, Andrew would never make a show of what he knows, yet his knowledge has deep ramification. He shares in his writings and teachings a great understanding of the care required to "build a world that includes a more compassionate relationship" not only with "the unwanted aspects of the self" as he puts it in *The Inner Studio*, but also, we could add, a more compassionate relationship with the repressed in history and in our societies. I love his description of the meaning of **understanding**: "seeing something from below, from a more humble, less power-centered vantage point, where one's previously held positions and opinions are less involved in the act of perception".

Andrew had a long-standing preoccupation with care, honoring what I am now thinking of as a form of prescience, an ability to see right through the things that must be done but also how they must be done—slowly, carefully, respectfully, yet with full and relentless dedication. Or perhaps this should more accurately be described as a **presence** rather than a prescience, a very involved presence that Andrew always adopted. He had the strength to be humble, the energy to be caring, the commitment to the now as a way of seeing further ahead, an attention to those around him as a way of effecting long-lasting and meaningful transformations.

Andrew's thoughtful advice, kind mentoring and caring presence was like a compass orienting so many students, colleagues, friends and the School of Architecture in fundamental ways. He was a wonderful thinker who quietly but unrelentingly put care in the center of so much of his work and teaching—and we are privileged to be able to continue to learn from him through *The Inner Studio*.

As to myself personally, I cannot begin to say how much I miss his guidance. He offered it always in a way that was so modest and self-effacing, dropping in to share a bit of advice before a retreat, to counsel on those messages which were the most difficult to write, or simply to humbly share views on some of those important conversations—conversations that are bound to always take place within a School filled with critical, creative, and passionate learners, teachers, and contributors.

Andrew, thank you. We miss you. You leave a gap that I do not believe anyone will ever be able to fill, but I find some solace in seeing so many students dedicating themselves to follow the path you helped them open up. Like them, we continue to learn from you as we aspire to be caring designers, determined listeners, and all around compassionate and empathetic colleagues, architects and citizens.

Anne Bordeleau
Director, School of Architecture, University of Waterloo
Cambridge, ON

Andrew Levitt quietly walked in and out of the Waterloo School of Architecture for over twenty years, transforming the lives of so many in his presence. At the heart of his teaching practice was the mantra: *may all students be successful*.

I had the privilege of being his student and seeing firsthand how his deep understanding of the inner world of a human being guided and ignited the creative potential of the design studio. Andrew taught that each student had a unique inner world that was inextricably linked to the meaning and outcomes of their creative work—a link that needed to be tended to with utmost care.

Care was at the core of Andrew's practice. He nurtured a space where all students in his presence were seen, heard, and cared for. His classroom and studio space transcended an intellectual experience, engaging the hearts, minds, hands, and feet of students in ways that left a lasting impression. In a world where we constantly look outward for answers and inspiration, Andrew enabled us to trust the innate wisdom of our creative instincts. In uncertainty, he encouraged us to listen from the tender place of our hearts, and live with questions instead of searching for immediate answers.

Like many students of Andrew, I carry his teaching with me. He offered more than a design education; he gave me a roadmap to better understand myself. The beauty of his book *The Inner Studio* is that it holds this very teaching: that we all have the inner know-how to be our true selves, and the creative capacity to imagine and create the best world for ourselves and those around us.

Jaliya Fonseka
Cambridge, ON

ACKNOWLEDGMENTS

This book has taken shape slowly over the last ten years through talks, seminars, and conversations, and I owe a great deal of thanks to many people. In particular, I want to thank the many students at the University of Waterloo School of Architecture whose imagination and determination inspired the core of this exercise.

I also want to express my sincere appreciation to those who encouraged me and helped drive this project forward. Among them, Ryszard Sliwka, Robert Van Pelt, Fred Thompson, Philip Beesley, Janna Levitt, and Tim Scott all made valuable contributions. Thanks also to Andrea Knight whose editing skillfully guided this book through to completion.

Finally, my heartfelt thanks go to Hannah, Josh, and Jake for their interest and enthusiasm, and to my wife, Wendy, whose love and support made this book possible.

Andrew Levitt (1953—2021)
2015

TABLE OF CONTENTS

Introduction

The Inner Studio is about learning to communicate from deep down in our imagination where creative instincts live and have meaning. It invites designers to trust the wisdom and creativity of their bodies, dreams, and shadows and bring these resources into the experience of design. Every creative process involves a dimension of pilgrimage. The Inner Studio sees the act of design as a special kind of school, a place of learning inside each of us where our relationship to creativity has the potential to teach us lessons about ourselves that are inseparable from what we build. This book is about the rich inner world of design.

Designers are people who feel passionately about the world, but rather than composing songs or writing novels, they express themselves by making decisions about the way material is organized, shaped, colored, and assembled. We cannot help ourselves. No item is too small to escape our eye and no event is too large to exceed our belief in the magical capacity of design to make a difference. Designers can be found everywhere–trying to improve cities, planning the way kitchens are arranged, thinking about the shapes of windows and the best material for a roof in the desert.

This book is for those of us who love design, who are fascinated by its problems and feel passionate about its possibilities. It is for professionals whose interest in architecture, landscape, interiors, graphics, or industrial design continues to grow and deepen, and for students who may feel both attracted to and surprised by design's powerful call. It is for people who want to express themselves through their environment and the decisions they make about the formal world. This book is for those who want to bring more of their inner world into the built world.

The idea of The Inner Studio grew out of my own realization that although we live in a world in which it is impossible to turn on the TV without hearing psychological discussions about adolescents, presidents, quarterbacks, or home renovations, our psychological awareness has not translated into a more inspired or compassionate built world.

Today a designer's education takes place in three places: in classrooms, where technical information is imparted; in professional offices, where students learn about real world practices; and in the design studio where creativity is cultivated and imagination is encouraged. Design students tend to practically live in "studio" and, while every school has unique and particular culture, the common element of studio life is comradeship and creative intensity. The culture within the studio may be driven by one powerful personality or a widely supported design ideal, but the rich and intimate job of relating, prioritizing, and reconciling the diverse experiences of creativity rests within each individual. I think of the place where these decisions are made as the "inner studio." *The Inner Studio* is where inspirations, imagination, longings, dreams, physical symptoms, intuitions, and design instincts arise and have their meaning. *The Inner Studio* is the place inside us that hosts our moments of discovery and elation and it is the place where we experience doubt and lose our resolve. It is the place inside us–*The Inner Studio*–that this book explores, validates, investigates, and celebrates. I hope that the approach of focusing on *The Inner Studio* encourages designers to experience the act of design as a process inseparable from enriching the self.

Architects have traditionally played a leading role in the design and building that shapes the world. It is true that this responsibility does not fall on their shoulders alone–it usually involves teams of professional colleagues such as highly skilled engineers, contractors, and other consultants who share in the considerable complexity, constraints, and liabilities–but it is difficult to imagine another profession that has the practical expertise, creative reach, theoretical understanding, and legal jurisdiction of modern architects when it comes to designing, shaping, and organizing the built world.

Why does *The Inner Studio* focus squarely on the act of design? Because the world we live in is now so exhaustively designed. The chair you are sitting in, the window you look through, the morning commute, the butter knife–beautiful or banal–all of these are the result of design. Anything that has been built has first been designed. Even those unbuilt places we cherish, such as wilderness areas, owe their continued existence to our capacity and intent to design and legislate for their survival. According to the World Watch Institute, by the end of this decade, for the first time, the majority of the earth's citizens will live in cities. This should give us pause.

Where we once lived in a symbiotic or harmonious relationship to our natural environment, today we live in a thoroughly built world in which we are rapidly losing the opportunity to gain the deeper self-knowledge that comes from observing the arising and passing away of natural things. Not only were we once part of nature, all the happenings of our inner world were considered "natural." How can self-knowledge be extracted from the designed environment unless the designers themselves can consciously experience their own inner worlds and use these to promote self-knowledge?

The purpose of psychology is to guide us through human problems and to help us make sense of our lives. Where we once prospered by studying the migration of animals, we now find ourselves struggling to know how we feel about ourselves and others. Clearly we live in a world that is both physical and psychological and we can no longer afford to leave out the complex, paradoxical, and often troublesome role of feelings that occur during the design process. Society has distinguished itself by its willingness to integrate new technologies—*The Inner Studio* proposes using the self-knowledge and creativity that reside in our modern understanding of the psyche.

Architects will often explain their work by saying that it has been "designed from within." This usually means that we are designing from some rational appreciation of a building's organization. I want to suggest a less intentional explanation, that there is a moment in the creative process that rests on a different kind of know-how, on the relationship we have to the inner world of our psyches. The role of inner know-how, the world of instinct, imagination, and intuition, the world of subtlety and felt sense, is not only a complementary counterweight to our technical training and practical skills, it also represents a part of ourselves that needs to be respected and developed and included in the built world.

The part of us that is at the undeclared center of creativity is outside most architectural curriculum, and it may seem odd to suggest that self-knowledge needs to become an integral part of a designer's education. But I find it very interesting that this undeclared inner world of the designer has always been covert and ignored in education. Schools make every investment in the outer world—becoming "wired," striving for enhanced global information exchanges, competing for academic excellence—and all of these are important, but they do not begin to address the deeper strata of conscious and unconscious longings, needs, emotions, and desires that influence decision makers and affect decision making. I have come to believe that the idea of declaring the role played by the psyche in the creation of the built world is the best way to guide architectural know-how and heal the environment. The revolution I am imagining is one where we step back and consider that learning how to face design problems is critically important in learning how to solve them, where we consider that the *how* can not be separated from the *what*.

While studying architecture in London, I often visited a public library on St. Martin's Street where I would spend time, reading, drawing, daydreaming, and wandering through the rich collection of books and journals. There was a modest scale to the three-story building and, sitting at a wooden desk in my favorite chair, I always felt comfortable, as though I was enjoying a stimulating conversation in the lobby of a small hotel. This was a library in which any idea could either be tracked back to its origins or projected into some future possibility.

One day I stumbled across an essay in *Art International* called "Suicide and the Soul" by the American psychologist James Hillman. I began reading and soon found myself completely immersed in the world of the psyche he described. I read late into the evening and returned to the library in the morning to finish the article before combing the bookshelves for works by Freud and Jung in order to better understand the essay. For the next week I returned every day to the library to read about the psyche. I moved from my usual chair in the art section to the psychology section of the library, and as I looked out a different window and studied from a new chair, it seemed to me that the very shape of the interior had somehow changed since my first visit to the building a year earlier. For an entire week I ate my lunch in the library and consumed everything I could find about the psyche until, without realizing it, something inside of me shifted and the mysterious dynamics of the unconscious took hold of me.

I remember leaving the library as it was closing, late in the afternoon of Christmas Eve, and walking up St. Martin's Street towards Leicester Square. The darkening street was filled with Londoners hurrying home or rushing to do last-minute shopping. Standing on the edge of Leicester Square, I stopped in the midst of this busy scene and suddenly felt something inside me open. I had always thought that London was very reserved and its citizens introverted, but now every face and every building seemed filled with inner stories and the world was somehow alive and freely expressing these hidden messages. Amazed, I felt as though I had slipped into a place that linked and underpinned the built world and the inner world. Ever since that moment, I have been trying to understand the practical lessons this experience has to offer.

Through the years that I worked as an architect, I continued my search. I spent 10 years exploring Buddhism and finally returned to school to study psychology and began working as a psychotherapist. I love architecture, but I carried within me a passion to understand the unseen side of things. It was that feeling that the world was made of two strands, the seen and unseen, that drew me to learn about the psyche and the role of the unconscious. I felt that architecture as it is generally practiced does not include the richness and complexity we see when we look at things psychologically, where mystery, uncertainty, or difficult conditions can surface and become integrated. With the built world, the provisional and irrational nature of things is seldom acknowledged. I felt I needed to enter and explore this aspect of the world. From architecture I learned how to look at the built world and something of the forces that shape it. From Buddhism I began to appreciate the depth of inner world. Finally, with psychology, I began to learn how our inner world and the built world are related.

Psychology has an enormous appetite for architectural language. Instead of using this language to describe physical things, psychology uses it to describe the psyche, the "place" where our conscious and unconscious mind are thought to reside. I began to wonder if the power and wonder of architectural phenomena rests in their ability to point to structures that reside in the immeasurable world of our psyche. In the world of the psyche, as in architecture, the primary dialogue concerns the relationship and boundary between inside and outside. Inner and outer may seek congruence or be split. Where inner and outer touch, psychology uses words like "façade," "boundary," "border," "threshold," and "wall." Psychologically speaking, walls may be transparent, rigid, divided, or fragile. Boundaries may be clear or need strengthening. They are subject to breaking down or may suffer a collapse, but they can also be rebuilt or repaired. Inside and outside are always interacting, and we depend on these invisible structures to make sense of the world. These psychic constructions may be functional or dysfunctional, they may feel heavy or light, or they may cause us to take flight, feel grounded, or feel out of place.

In the psychological world we commonly describe our moods with reference to space. "I'm feeling down," "I'm feeling up," "She's beside herself with anger," "You're driving me up the wall," "She's feeling open" or "He's always closed down." We have an innate sense of ourselves as the "center" and use symbolic ideas about place to help us communicate our moods. We have established, through descriptions of psychological space, experiences that we bring to the built world.

Psychological language has moved quickly into every corner of our conversations because we need its capacity for describing the immeasurable yet tactile experience of moods. Words like "split," "compensation," "sublimation," "fragments," "nightmare," "light" and "shadow" are found in descriptions of both the built world and therapeutic case histories. They have been absorbed into architecture with the meaning acquired in psychological discourse.

The education of designers currently begins and ends with the rational world. We might believe that this was sufficient if we did not have the evidence of a troubling state of affairs in the built world. What is missing from the built world is what is missing from the education of the designer: a more conscious agreement to include the energy, mystery, and imagination of our inner world in the process of design.

I experienced great difficulties when I began studying psychology because the skills I needed to develop did not come naturally and always seemed to evaporate when I reached for them. This experience of learning to wrestle with what I found overwhelming and difficult was the training that allowed me to help others. When I began teaching design to architecture students I felt that I had something to offer beyond design skills. I knew the psychological value of wrestling and learning from mistakes. I began to appreciate how psychological questions and issues of self-expression swirl at the heart of every creative project. Making these moments more conscious was the way to move through them and the only way to avoid unconsciously projecting them out onto individuals, communities, even whole cultures. I saw that I could teach design as a process of enriching both the designer and the world. This book gives new tools to those who want to more deeply trust and explore their creative instincts. I hope that placing the spotlight on our inner resources can help bring the creativity and wisdom of our inner world to the built world.

PART ONE

The Inner World
of the Psyche

Why is it that we can easily arrange to have a coffee at 11 am, but we can never arrange to have a creative insight at 2 pm? Why can we plan with some certainty to have a holiday in March, but we cannot plan with any certainty to have a dream tonight? To plan a vacation, we need to do research, make bookings, clear our schedules. It is far less clear how to marshal the necessary inner resources–intuition, imagination, and insight–required to fulfill a creative project. To understand this dynamic more fully we need to explore the inner world of the psyche and, in particular, the relationship between the ego and the unconscious.

We need a strong ego because it gives us a healthy sense of who we are, which in turn gives us the confidence to go after the things we want. But when it comes to creativity, the role of the ego changes. Creativity is not something we can simply go out and get–it is something we receive, and this can only happen when the ego surrenders enough to let the creative spirit come through. Since the divine or creative spirit is outside of our control, it is not surprising that we become stuck when we focus on the ego as the vehicle for creativity. Although the ego does decide how much of the divine comes through and can bring structure and preferences to the creative process, a strong ego alone can never guarantee whether we will be blessed when we undertake creative work. This explains why relaxation–even a kind of self-forgetfulness–so often accompanies the creative experience, as do daydreaming, reverie, play, and an unfettered imagination. How does the inner world of the psyche facilitate and support the creative experience of the designer?

Unconscious

By the end of the 19th century, Western science had largely finalized and systematized descriptive human anatomy. No sooner had the relationships and functioning of our physical anatomy been completed then another complex aspect of human beings began to receive the attention of scientists. This new exploration did not concern itself with the role of the spleen, femur, and liver, but with the ego, shadow, and dreams. In particular, the pioneers of psychology such as Freud, Adler, and Jung began to grapple with the role of the unconscious and an understanding of the psyche that could explain and systematize human behavior. One hundred years of studying psychology has resulted in a fundamental shift in the way we imagine ourselves and the way we explain our actions. We no longer see ourselves as possessing only a physical body; it is now widely understood that we also possess a psychic body with its own unique relationships and anatomy. The discovery of the modern idea of this psyche not only gave us a new vocabulary with which to describe and understand our thoughts, feelings, and actions, it made us aware that our physical and psychic bodies are so interconnected that science increasingly suggests that they are best understood as single interdependent entities. We all belong not only to the world of form, but also to the formless world of the psyche.

If the physical brain can be understood as being made up of different parts, so too can its psychological counterpart, the mind. The following diagram is drawn from the work of Carl Jung, whose explorations of the psyche form the cornerstone of the inner studio. It outlines a psychological model of a human being, what the psyche would look like if we could simplify its contents to the clarity of a diagram. It represents human psychological anatomy that is composed of two different but interdependent worlds: the conscious mind and the unconscious mind. The circle is used symbolically to convey the idea of being whole. It is the Self–the sum total of all the psychic entities and elements of which we are made.

Think of this diagram as a map of the psyche that helps us name and orient ourselves to the unseen forces that affect our lives.

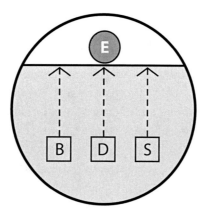

PSYCHE

We can all point to where we live on the map of our city; psychology allows us to point to where we may find our self in the rich dynamic world of the psyche.

Above the line, is the world where we are conscious and our ego is in command. The ego is the aspect of our psyche that helps us make decisions. It helps us get from A to B, to choose coffee or tea, whether to wear sandals or shoes, and when to go to bed. It governs all that we are conscious of and it follows that we need a strong ego to be happy in the world. Yet when the ego exerts too much control, we may find ourselves unable to adapt or learn and are seen as "egotistical." This "strength" can cause all sorts of problems. A simple example is a situation in which we are so certain of our position that we can't listen to other opinions. Having a healthy ego would allow us to admit that we are lost and ask for directions.

Paradoxically, while the ego has the job of defending our self-interest and helping us to make choices, psychological growth comes from allowing what is below the line, below the threshold of consciousness, to come to consciousness. In other words, to grow, create, and mature, the ego must learn to let go and surrender so that something new and creative can happen. And the new thought, inspiration, or insight has its source in the unconscious. While we usually prefer to feel in charge and able to control things, the diagram suggests that there are many times in life and during the creative process when letting go of the ego-held position is the way forward.

When we start a creative project the role of our ego is to establish a structure that best supports us in finding a creative solution. For example, we may decide to work on the project at 2 pm for 30 minutes. We may wish to have our door open or closed, to listen to music or be in silence, to study the work of other designers or concentrate on a particular or general aspect of our problem–all of these decisions are in the hands of the ego and all contribute to creating the most fertile circumstances for receiving the creative impulse. But because the ego does not have the "answer" to the creative problem, once we establish the creative environment all we can do is begin our work with patience and faith that the creative spirit or divine will come through. We can no more force creative states to appear than we can force someone to love us. The truth is that we never know if we will be visited with an new inspiration, sudden intuition, or powerful image. We need to diminish the role of the ego but not lose control. The ego gives us our structure, but the outcome is always unknown to us.

The horizontal line that divides the circle represents the threshold of awareness. It is the boundary between the conscious and unconscious. Our experience of the transformation that is possible when psychic contents move from unconscious to conscious explains why the idea threshold is such an important experience in the built world. An example of the power of this can be seen in the three quotes that Jung had carved in the places that held great significance for him. On the stone lintel above the front door of his house at Kusnacht is carved *Vocatus atque non vocatus deus aderit*– "Invited or not the gods are present." Over the fireplace at his retreat in Bollingen is carved *Quero quod impossible*–"Seek that which is not possible." Finally, *Vocatus atque non vocatus deus aderit*–"Invited or not the gods are present"–reappears on another threshold between worlds: Jung's tombstone.

Standing at the threshold is a very creative place to be. The ability to straddle two worlds is something we can experience through creativity, dreaming, active imagination, drawing, and physical movement. Developing the ability to receive, trust, and work with these inner messages takes practice. Some may favor working with dreams; for others, the body may be the vehicle. The act of creative design means learning how to receive, participate, and ground the messages that come from the unconscious. We are usually so identified with the ego that we falsely believe it is responsible for everything that happens to us; when we actually have to create something, we discover its limitations. The ego itself is really more of an administrator that initiates circumstances. When we want to be creative we are really looking for a divine gift, a blessing or a message from the unconscious. To be in a creative state is to be at one with something greater than ourselves. This means that the delicate play between our egos and the mysterious forces of the unconscious really determines how much of the creative impulse or divine we can receive.

The area below the horizontal line on the diagram line represents the personal unconscious, all the things we are not conscious of that have the possibility of bringing new understanding and growth to our lives. Although it is often characterized as negative or even pathological, the unconscious is in fact the source of much that is positive. It represents the unlimited potential of things. It has the flavor of eternity: it is unknowable, which is to say it is inexhaustible. The more we know of it the greater it becomes. Its discovery by Western science changed forever our experience of being human because it brought the unknown squarely "inside" us. Our sense of belonging in the world has never been the same.

A Jungian analyst from Canada, Darryl Sharp, defines the unconscious in the following way:

> The unconscious is:
> Everything I know, but which at the moment I am not thinking of.
> Everything I was once conscious of, but have now forgotten.
> Everything perceived by my senses but not noted by my conscious mind.
> Everything that I feel, think, remember, want, and do; all the future things that are taking shape in me and will some time come to consciousness involuntarily without my paying attention to it.

The unconscious points to and is the experience of "unknown" forces, inspirations, hunches, and creations that seem to come from somewhere outside of us and push their way into our conscious mind. Three significant aspects of the unconscious psyche that we need to examine in greater detail are dream, body, and shadow.

The body is often thought of as conscious—after all, it is visible, we can touch it. But when we look at it more closely, it is clear that the body actually exists in two worlds. We do not consciously instruct our bodies to taste or to see, and the secretions of our livers or spleens happen far below the threshold of consciousness. Yet we may get ill just before an important presentation, or we may find ourselves inexplicably exhausted after a visit with a friend. Through various symptoms, the body can make the unconscious known to us.

Dreams are those recollected narratives that we are conscious of when we awake up. Their content cannot be controlled any more than their recollection can be guaranteed. They represent an unconscious snapshot of our circumstances. When we go to sleep the ego is no longer present. But if, when we awake, we can recall the dream we are able to incorporate and learn from the point of view of the unconscious. Dreams speak to us through symbols.

Shadow is a Jungian term pointing to that "darker" part of ourselves that we are not proud of or a positive aspect that we have difficulty accepting. In either case the shadow will create difficulties for us and for those around us. Think of the shadow as the underbelly of our spiritual nature, with qualities such as greed, hatred, and narcissism. Our difficulty in accepting these qualities usually results in statements and actions through which we unconsciously project these unwanted "unacceptable" characteristics onto others—or onto our designs for the built world. The benefit of the dynamic of projection is that it allows us to become aware of these otherwise hidden aspects of ourselves.

The arrows in the diagram are very important. They indicate the energy inside every psychic transaction that constantly pulls matter toward greater consciousness and light. As Jung wisely observed, the reason why consciousness exists is simply that without it things go less well. While it is true that consciousness does make things better, it is important to point out that difficulties, trials, and hardship play an important role in maturing the ego. The drive to become more conscious may be inevitable and long-standing, but it can also be extremely confusing and often disagreeable. The tension that can build between the ego (rushing in to find an answer) and the unconscious (vague signals of not being ready) often results in considerable anguish and confusion. Our ability to hold the tension of these opposites becomes the energetic source that empowers a creative breakthrough. The creative impulse often impels us to break a rule or expectation. Listening to the messages from your body, dream, and shadow that illuminate your path or give you direction can often support you in having the courage to stay true to your creative instinct. What makes it possible for us to redeem and make sense of this process is psychology. Psychology has become popular because it helps individuals take responsibility for their fates. If the last century established the reality of the unconscious, I hope that the next 100 years will grow our ability to relate to its contents.

As designers, and as individuals, we want to have a healthy working relationship with the part of our psyche that is below the line, the place where our creative resources live. We want to develop a curiosity, respect, and ability to work with the signals that comes from below. No matter how aware we become, the knowledge that there is an everlasting supply of creativity and insight from the unconscious–that indeed these two worlds are forever dependent on one another–is one of the most precious gifts of being human. In the course of designing we often find ourselves unwilling to change something that has caused us to remain stuck. It is useful to remember that the psyche is dynamic and constantly changing. Growth means change. If there was no change we would not be able to grow up and realize our hopes and dreams.

Although the concept of the unconscious may now be widely accepted, we have made much less progress in incorporating and relating to what comes out of our unconscious. So far we have given far greater attention to striving for perfection than getting to know the paradoxical and imperfect nature of our own psyches.

While many theorists say that the modern period is over, I disagree. Given the enormous and hugely difficult labor involved in becoming conscious, it's more likely that modernism is still in its earliest stages. The discovery of the unconscious was radical and important because it shifted the focus of the creative act to the individual. We finally have a map that shows the individual as something beyond flesh and blood. We are just beginning to learn to truly live as individuals in the center of things conscious and unconscious. What will happen when we begin to design the built world from a place that accepts responsibility for the existence of the conscious and the unconscious worlds?

Calling on the Unconscious in Design

The Designer's Journal

Journaling is a reflective method of recording your experience. It encourages subjectivity and focuses on the development and expression of the designer's true voice through two different approaches.

The first involves keeping a written log, a design journal that reports on the way that you experience the process of design. This commentary records not only the feelings and thoughts, intuitions and understandings that arise during the design process, but records when these experiences arise. This journal seeks to help you identify your moods, likes, and dislikes, and find their correlation with your difficulties and pleasures.

As an experiment, try writing at the same time every day and simply describe what is happening inwardly as you make your way through the cycles of design. What made you feel confident and what made you lose your way? Where is your excitement and where do you find yourself withdrawing or feeling a sense of dread? Use this record to develop an awareness of and a respect for your creative self.

The second form of the design journal is also subjective, but brings together text and drawings. It may be thought of as almost a travel diary. The journey that is being described is a spontaneous record of how the built world is moving you, what you like and dislike, what opens you and what causes you to shut down. To do this, it is important that you draw first and describe later. In this format the journal seeks to turn the ordinary into the extraordinary though your capacity to pay attention to your design instincts and reflexes. This journal rests on the transcription of drawings and experience, so it asks you to bring your eye, hand, and sense of self into a flexible, unified trio that is willing to learn from the subjective experience of perception.

With both of these approaches the key is learning to express what is happening inwardly. This is a private record of what is moving you in the built world, a tool that will help you develop a more robust and agile sense of your design voice.

Visiting Places

When I first visited Italy, I was surprised by the way people filled the public spaces of the towns and cities. Where I come from, people think of the city only as a place to move through, and because they feel consistently frustrated in their efforts to do this, the city is always being blamed. Every rush hour the traffic report describes the city as a failure because our desire to get somewhere is constantly being thwarted. Cities become the cause of our lateness, the reason why we are stuck sitting in cars. The city won't let us move. In reality, nothing could be further from the truth.

In Rome there is no hope of moving easily through the city. Everyone knows this. Everyone knows that this is not what cities are for. They are not for moving through–they are for being in. In Rome I saw people who knew instinctively how to be in a space and I wanted to join them. They were standing in public places, in streets, plazas, doorways, balconies, near fountains under loggias, on steps. I wondered, Where did they learn this? Everyone–men and women, young and old–seem to just know what cities are for. They are standing alone or in groups, talking, looking, whistling, smoking, eating, congregating. They have all acquired some basic skill for being in space. They know what it feels like to have their bodies in space. They know what space is for. It's not just for us to move through, but to be in. To enjoy the sense of being physically included. I could see how gracefully people stood in space. They gestured and talked or read the paper, but mostly they seemed naturally confident in their bodies' position in the space. Even the clothes they wore seemed designed for this purpose. They seemed to know that being in space is a sensual experience.

> I wanted to understand the role design played in their knowing. A non-smoker, I bought a pack of cigarettes so I would have something to do, walked out into the middle of public space, and lit a cigarette. Then I noticed the oversized human figures. In every public place, planted in space, naked or draped, human or mythological, stood magnificent stone figures. I began to wonder if these were the teachers that mentored everyone. If you can't be Marcus Aurelius, you can at least stand like him. These statues, with all their passion, expression, and quite literally larger-than-life drama, were introducing us to the idea of being in space and expressing our selves. They also make it impossible to feel alone in space. They offer a very physical gift that ensures the place you are entering is full before you arrive. There is no chance of being alone or the first one to the party. Yes, there are spaces devoted to different purposes, such as markets or religious spaces or cafés, but beneath this level of purpose is the sensual experience of trusting your body in space. Italian clothing seems more draped for standing in than fitted for action. Posture, gesture, repose, waiting, walking, watching, and talking take on special importance in public space. Space is for being in. Space is for occupying. It's the message from the humanist space age. The piazza is a great classroom—it teaches us how to hold our ground in the world. This knowledge is transferred out to streets and lesser places. Great cities are designed for being in, not moving through.

When we try to build new piazzas in North America we forget to include these instructions. We build public space but forget to tell people what it's for. Why would we go there? In North America we are trained by design decisions that places are for doing something.

When it comes to new spaces we are not told how to do our part. We can't stand there because we believe cities are for moving through. Space is for filling. It makes us feel vulnerable and wrong to go against the purpose of the city: Every message is about doing something and being somewhere and suddenly we are expected to take a 10-minute holiday in the middle of space. This is not possible. We need to include the subtle instructions and guidance that design is capable of expressing. But we don't build the instructions any more. Great design always brings these subtle instructions. The lessons are not written out but conveyed by a skillful combination of immanence and scale.

The other reason that we have had so many problems designing modern public spaces is that we have left the modern human anatomy of the psyche out of the equation. We need to make places that speak to our conscious and unconscious mind. Modern public space is disappearing because we stopped including the experience of being a modern human being; we excluded our psychological world from space-making. Public space actually lost its constituency: the modern public. As a result, a population that was born into the era of the unconscious, with it's anxiety, depression, and shadow has not been given a place to go, a place to recognize and belong in, a public space, for example, that encourages people who feel isolated to come together. The invention of perspective changed the built world as did a new understanding of the orbit of the planets. We are waiting for a rebirth of the design of cities and architecture that acknowledges the existence of the psyche.

Today we might expect to see architects plumbing the depths, richness, vitality, and sometimes disturbing moods of the modern psyche, with all its shadow-soaked complexes, in order to give public space its modern character. While public space did not traditionally concern itself with the shadow, it could be said that the world of psychology and the shadow have never been so available for discussion. A truly contemporary public space, one that engages the richness of soul, might give expression to a psychological victory such as reconciliation with oneself. A new commission for a modern public space, for example, might ask designers to create a public space that makes room for the shadow.

EXERCISE

Find a place where you can walk without being interrupted. This could be inside your home or in a park or on the street where you live. Start by standing still for a moment and let your gaze fall on a distant object–this may be a wall 30 feet away or the mailbox on the corner. Now begin to walk at a relaxed pace toward the object, but as you approach the object become aware of your desire to get there. There is no need to worry, you will get there if for no other reason then you are walking in that direction, but the high level of inner verbal traffic, planning, and preparations that arises in your mind may surprise you. Let your gaze rests on the object you are approaching and just quietly remind yourself to let go of the desire to comment on the inevitable. We all carry a tremendous energy called desire. To get somewhere is to accomplish something. To reach a goal is fundamental and necessary and woven very deeply into our existence. However during this experiment when your mind begins racing toward the object, just return to the sensation of being with your body and the sensation of walking. This exercise offers a brief glimpse of how our desire to get something or get somewhere often comes at the expense of being present. Creativity is an experience that happens naturally when we are living in the present, not busy planning the future or worrying about the past.

PART TWO

The Creative Instinct

When I was very young, my favorite dessert was pound cake. Whenever it was served I would rush into the kitchen to get a small knife that was ideal for carving. My mother would call out, "Andrew, please eat your dessert," but I would pretend to not hear her so I could concentrate on sculpting my piece of cake into a building. The cake was soft but firm, perfect for carving. No doubt spurred on by the reward of eating it, I savored every moment of being absorbed in these dinner table creations.

Jung believed that every human being has five instincts: to create; to search for meaning; aggression; sex; and to satisfy hunger. The idea of an instinct is that it does not arise in the intellect, even though it may seem like a thought. An instinct is an energetic impulse that fuses the body and mind into a single entity. An example of the creative instinct happens to me whenever I drive through Arizona. At some point I suddenly turn to my wife and say, "Stop the car! I need to take a photograph!" It's the same energy that drives you buy a guitar or reach for a tall glass of water after a long workout. Jung's observations were based not just on the people around him, but on what individuals have done over thousands of years. The need to create, to search for meaning, to satisfy an empty stomach, to act impulsively, or to reach out for another human being have been moving human beings since the beginning of time. The urge to create is to the psyche what the urge to eat is to the body. Instincts transcend nationalities or race. They are root experiences of being alive and their energy is familiar to everyone. This helps explain why we experience such as a crisis when we are creatively blocked. When an instinct is blocked, the energy of our lives is disrupted and we feel dispirited.

Four Reflections on Being Creative

The conditions, experiences, and relationships that we find when we look at the inner world of the designer are called reflections because they are intended to be reflected upon. They are not rules; they are tools for awakening and strengthening design instincts and they point us toward the underlying dynamic stages of the design experience. I invite you to explore your own creative instincts by reflecting on the characteristics I have observed in the design studio. They are intended as centering devices to help you contend with the mind-numbing number of complexities that can occupy designers when they enter into the process of designing.

There can be no better way for a designer to come to know his or her inner world than to reflect inwardly while moving through the stages of design. Designers process enormous amounts of information, both consciously and unconsciously, on their way to producing a design. On one hand they must deal with regulations, dimensions, performance standards, clients' needs, and so on. On the opposite hand, designers receive images, signals, and inspirations from the world of imagination, with its mysterious layers and the feelings of things only faintly seen. Our ability to stand at the center of these two worlds and not get caught in either, to work with both, makes us modern.

Let's look at the trajectory of how an idea develops. When deconstructed and described, the inner states that constitute a methodology of design may seem familiar because we are so intimately involved with them. But we may not be aware of their significance. By slowing down automatic or habitual practices we can locate ourselves in the design process and reflect on our relationship to the subtle forces that move our design work.

I have always had to use diagrams to help me think. Whenever I find myself puzzled or facing a complicated situation I make a diagram and in the course of creating the diagram I often uncover a solution to the problem. This diagram is the result of trying to explain to myself and to others the experience of design. I use it like a map and as a way of reflecting on the mystery and power of the creative experience. I hope it helps you contend with the

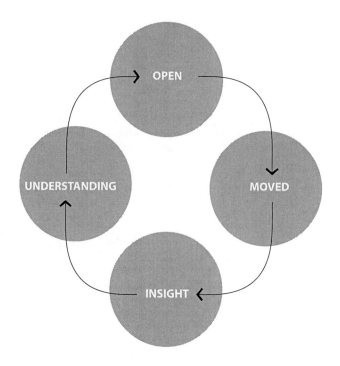

FOUR REFLECTIONS

complexities that can easily overwhelm designers when they enter into the creative process.

These four reflections—openness, being moved, insight, and understanding—are arranged in a wheel to suggest their cyclic and interdependent relationship. But in practice, things are not so simple. These four reflections can as easily be stages in a process as interdependent factors forming a wheel that starts to spiral as we ascend or descend through the design journey. Like eddies in a stream they may form larger or smaller moments as you move through a creative project. Being aware of where you are in this wheel will help you concentrate the internal resources, energies, and attitudes that best serve you.

Openness

This is the first and most difficult pre-condition for creativity. It is first because in order to create, you have to be able to receive, and in order for you to be receptive, you have to risk being vulnerable. To be open means letting go of self-judgment and criticism and just allowing something to happen. It means being willing to learn from what you encounter. If you are open, anything can happen. Most importantly, the unexpected has a chance to enter. If you are overly judgmental or critical of yourself you will find that you rarely feel inspired and the process of creativity becomes a burden.

The experience that I find closest to the start of a creative project is the experience of traveling. What I enjoy most about traveling is the experience of arrival, the first moment in a new place, when my senses are in a state of high alert. There is an excitement in the air, the excitement of discovery. A sight, sound, or fragrance may lead to something. A glance from a stranger or the way the light falls on a street may lead to wonderful discoveries. Places like Kyoto or the Grand Canyon are called "great" because they have the power to bring us into the present moment. Their beauty unifies our body and mind and opens us to wonder. In the presence of great places we are intensely exposed to the power of awareness and the arising and passing away of things that move us.

Like a traveler, a designer arriving in front of a new project wants to be open to receiving new and unexplored impressions, images, sights, sounds, and smells of a new place. The senses are our faithful helpers, tirelessly bringing us the world. The reason we need to experience openness is that it directly affects our capacity to connect to the world. And being open to the built world prepares us for our other, less-discussed job–being open to our own thoughts, feelings, and intuitions. To be "modern" means we have no choice but to be working with the totality of the psyche, assimilating what is outside us and what is inside us. We want to be able to work in both of these dimensions, learning how inner and outer phenomena affect us. But rather than helping us open up, much of the built world invites us to shut down, which makes it even more difficult to be open to our inner voices and impulses.

The elusive world of interior signals such as intuitions, dreams, and instincts is easily ignored, but these subtle and sometimes delicate images and voices have much to teach us. On one level they heighten our capacity to relate to the world and to ourselves; on another they also promise something positive and important to the environment. Learning to value our own sensitivity opens the door to creating built places that will do the same for everyone who encounters them. Experiencing ourselves more richly will change the world as we create more places for people to belong and feel at home with their inner experience. As we bring our openness to the world, it is hard not to be struck by how overwhelming and under-nourishing much of our built world has become.

At its most subtle level, openness offers us the potential of looking directly at our relationship to what is around us. When we are open, we are not trying to get anything, we are trying simply to be with something or someone. We are not competing with anyone or pursuing a goal. Our attention is open and resting with the object, whether it is internal or external. Does our usual way of looking involve trying to get something from the object? The energy required to sustain an attitude of "getting something" will affect, paradoxically, what we can see and what we are able to receive. When we are simply seeing, immersed in seeing, we can make contact with what we are observing. Taking an uninterrupted, sustained, steady look at something means allowing whatever our senses encounter to exist, churn, or play until the current of energy that accompanies the experience is finished.

One way to experience this is to take a few breaths, close your eyes, and allow your attention to settle on an awareness of your body. Allow your body to answer the question "How am I feeling?" Then open your eyes and bring the quality of your answer to whatever your eye falls on.

Though it may sound simple, this takes practice. Most of our seeing is so overlaid with opinions and rushing to know and acquire that the moments of pure seeing are few. Openness enables us to simultaneously take in and explore the quality of what is before us and what is inside us. We have to be mindful of balancing perception and comprehension. Too much concentration, and openness will suffer. Too much openness, and there is a lack of focus. Looking at a flower is a good way to practice being open. If you find you are too concentrated, allow the looking to come from your whole body. Can you look at the flower with an open body? What about being open to other, more mysterious phenomena, such as the night sky? What about being open to learning from a dream, or perhaps the symptoms from your body? We want to get to know the feeling of being open so that we can learn how to use our inner and outer circumstances to support our creativity.

Students of art, architecture, and design may work in a studio, but having a creative attitude means looking at the entire world as your studio. Everything you encounter—the taste of jam, the way shadows mark a wall, the chance remark of a friend, your curiosity about bicycles—everything you are open to has the potential to become part of your creative transformation. The ability to be open means you have enrolled in the classroom of life and are willing to learn from the way the phenomena of the world affect your body and mind.

Kyoto

In Japan the instructions about our relationship to space are not transmitted in public piazzas but in gardens. The Japanese are less concerned with the lessons of being in space than they are with the lessons of being present, less concerned with our position in the external world than with our relationship to our inner world. Japanese gardens are filled with objects such as gates, trees, plants, and stones, but rarely are you encouraged to move along a path. All points seem equal, as though it is more important to be present than to get somewhere. The hierarchy of external things is undone and you feel guided to observe your own mind. To be in the middle of things is to be centered in your own body and mind. A garden devoted to reflecting the nature of the mind, the expecting, reject-ing, assuming, rejoicing, and starting-again mind. It must be spacious to be able to hold so much conflict, so many memories and opinions. There is nothing to do in these gardens. Nothing is being sold. Nothing is blinking the latest stock market quotes. This is empty-space instruction. Not being encouraged to move subtly works to stop some modest level of attachment in your busy mind. Gradually, a balance of fullness and restraint draws you inward. With such a deep sense of choice about where your attention might rest, all things seem to return you to your own mind. The garden has become a mirror of your thoughts and a setting that encourages honest observation. Inhaling, you are looking at the garden. Exhaling, you feel yourself beginning to settle into the moment. Inhaling, you are trying to make opinions stay. Exhaling, you see that they just want to come and go. The garden is less in front of you and you are in more in it.

> *The day I went to visit Ryokanji, I made sure I arrived very early in the morning. I was waiting at the gate when a monk appeared and, with a nod, opened the door. I walked quickly up the stone steps toward my favorite garden. As I grew closer I realized I was alone and slowed down. At the first glimpse, I was transfixed. I remember inhaling as an image of the place entered me. Then, exhaling, I slowly felt the effort of the morning commute disappear and I entered the place again, as though for a second time, feeling more physically settled, shoulders dropping, a tremor of being at one with the place. Then another inhalation and a journey without words took place through years of expectations and opinions and then, finally, exhaling and feeling present. A moment later, brilliant laughter as a hundred young school children ran into the temple, thrilled to have a morning out of the classroom.*

Being Moved

If you are open to the world, you will be moved. And if you are moved, it means you have the capacity to receive inspiration, you have made a personal connection with something. The feeling of being moved is a precious and exciting moment in the journey toward self-expression. If we allow ourselves to be moved, we have the opportunity to learn about the power of artifacts, places, and landscapes to affect and motivate us. If we are not open, we will not be moved and it will be a mighty struggle to create anything. The reason a creative experience feels so good is that when we feel moved by creative energy we feel whole, for a brief moment we are at one with the creative spirit. We don't want anything because we feel as though we have everything. We can get this feeling from seeing great art, being at one with another, experiencing a sublime view of the Pacific Ocean, achieving a breakthrough in a difficult negotiation, or resolving a creative project.

Being moved can also be extremely subtle and take place over time. It can take the form of realizing that a breeze has cooled us or it can be a silent wave of joy when we stand in a place we have dreamed of occupying. It can as easily come from within us as from outside of us. Dreams, images, and ideas are potentially charged with an ability to move us, though these phenomena are free of any visible substance. It is said that Irish music can make us dance, make us cry, make us laugh, or put us to sleep. Anything has the power to move us if we are willing to be open. Even in its most basic iteration, we move toward what we like and avoid what we don't like. We are always living with the opportunity to learn about the power of things to move us.

When we are moved we are participating more than intellectually. Creativity comes in part directly from the intimately physical experience of being moved. We need this initial personal relationship with what we are creating to help us feel involved with our work as it develops. In time, these feelings are transformed into buildings, bridges, coffee shops, and parks that are capable of containing human feelings.

I sat down at Maggie's desk to begin the design tutorial. We had already met several times during the term to talk about her project for a new inner city neighborhood that would accommodate close to 12,000 people. She hadn't finished the project, but she had been working hard, and, with only three weeks left in the term, unfinished parts of the project naturally needed to be resolved. I was surprised to hear her say she felt she needed to start over. She gave a list of reasons: other people didn't like her project, she felt she had lost contact with the design she had originally wanted to do, and she didn't feel happy. She said everyone was telling her to do something different. To me, the project seemed promising, more in need of determination then demolition, more in need of steadiness then criticism.

I said, "Design is easier when you feel moved. Is there anything you feel a need to include in this project? It helps when you create what you love..." and then Maggie began to cry. We were sitting in the middle of a large and busy studio. I asked her if she was okay. She said yes, but she had been barely sleeping because she had been working so hard and that she was very tired. She drank some water and I asked her if she wanted to take a walk or talk outside. She said no and as she continued to cry, she began to draw. As she drew, she apologized for crying and began to show me tiny sketches of the ideas she wanted to include in the project. Ideas of canals and walking trails that would break down the massive housing blocks she had started with and didn't like. As she cried, described, and sketched, a new layer of the project emerged, something more alive, delicate, less rigid, and more sensitive. She kept apologizing for her tears and soon her vision was clear.

I could feel that somehow the project had been taken over by some part of her trying to please others. And I don't mean the 12,000 future inhabitants. I mean all the power-laden voices of authority she had always interacted with. To imagine this project more richly, to put herself wholeheartedly into this project, Maggie needed to retrieve and trust her own creative instincts. This project, although a community for 12,000 residents, was also a very personal project. Her inner world–maybe even her own soul–was very involved in the design process. This is true to a greater or lesser degree for all designers on every project, and it is particularly true in the process that is used to teach designers. Our capacity to feel as though we belong in the world–indeed our capacity to design a compassionate world–depends upon our ability to bring our souls safely into the world.

Maggie was able to re-organize her project around her true desires for the city and in the end her project managed to reflect and integrate her new confidence and a level of subtlety that was widely appreciated. Her final project did not win the highest grade, but she was more than pleased with her work. Years later she told me that this project had been the true start of her education *because it marked the beginning of her commitment to her creative instincts. She had learned to trust herself, to trust her creative instincts, to make contact with her inner studio.*

The inner studio is inside every designer; it is where the act of designing occurs. The inner world of the designer is where he or she searches, probes, filters, and encourages dialogues, and creates images. It is a place as vast and rich as the universe. It contains our imagination and doubts; it holds our heart's desires and our memories; it is full of conscious and unconscious thoughts. In this covert world the designer talks directly with the images, listens to whispers and memories, receives inspiration and hunches, and experiences the reveries that go into the creation of things. The sacred studio is the inner world of the psyche that offers its resources to the designer. Our relationship to this world offers humanizing and transforming insight to design. It is a place of transformation for both the designer and the built world.

To arrive at this studio, you need only arouse the intention to design. Your eyes may be open or closed. You have only to inwardly ask a question and material may begin to flow from unseen sources to consciousness. This place inside us–constantly traveled yet untouched, constantly there, but not easy to find–is where the making of the world begins and is consciously or unconsciously decided. Our job as designers is to learn how to connect with this inner world, how to contain it and work with it, how to activate it, listen to it, and finally befriend it. This is a special skill, one that we can become conscious of and develop.

The inner world is subtle. Its rules and rituals are different from those in the built world. When your car is stuck in the snow, a few strong friends can push it out; it's not as easy to get pushed out of a creative block. Physical laws do not govern this realm. We need to recognize the new rituals and rhythms that operate when we begin to move inwardly. We need to be willing to allow ourselves to be moved for two reasons. First, so we can get to know what it is like to surrender in the moment and, second, so that we have something to analyze. I want to leave some breadcrumbs along the trail so we can experience these two movements.

Design What You Love: Our Hearts' Desires

The course of true love
Never did run smooth.
–William Shakespeare

A designer who wishes to learn from and about the creative process begins the process of design by connecting with his or her heart's desire. What exactly is our heart's desire? It is whatever moves us. It may be a feeling, a memory, a love of dancing or cooking. It may be sparked by the sensation of a material, a conversation, a film, or a chance encounter. It is the energy that supports our creative instincts and a constant source of guidance during the process of design. Whatever we believe passionately and feel is true, wherever we feel our interest, curiosity, or enthusiasm–there we find our heart's desire. It may be our love of Prada handbags or long bicycle trips. It may be a fascination with sculpture or it may be a curiosity about the distance between people when they communicate. Our heart's desire is the courage and resolve behind our imagination and the unlikely source for the discipline and guidance required for the realization of our work.

While great visions are not common and can never be controlled, the ability to respond, honor, and commit to our heart's desire is always available to us. The energy of these desires carries the possibility of transformation. Ultimately every designer is involved in transforming spirit into matter. This movement deepens with trust and over time becomes the foundation that anchors and feeds our design instincts.

When we begin a new project, we are searching for a starting point. We are looking for inspiration, a transcendent idea, or an insight that will give our project its structure, vision, and power to move us and touch others. We are searching for a source that will give the design its sense of identity and presence. Over time we learn that this starting point can be modest–it does not have to be perfect. Its job is to launch the design enterprise. The starting point will transform as we go through the challenges that are common to every project.

What is most important is to trust our heart's desire to connect us with the vibrant and rich source of images and creative instincts that are needed in the built world. Spirit without matter leaves us with ghostly places, while the unrelenting world of matter without a higher purpose leaves us feeling alone in a banal environment. The idea that launches a project has great importance to designers and society. Our heart's desire has the power to transform what begins in the mind into something that can help and inspire others.

In the beginning, you may experience confusion about what constitutes your heart's desire. Although the designer in you has been moved, you still may be more focused on comparing yourself to others or even devaluing your own experience. My experience is that everyone has their own unique way of being creative. When a number of people visit the same place there are always multiple stories to tell. Someone may bring back a sketch, someone else may bring back a stone. Another person may relate a memory that was triggered. Someone may be amazed by the way the light struck a branch. Any experience can form the seed that moves us.

Where does a creative instinct come from? No one knows exactly, but we all know how to ask for help. And this capacity to sincerely ask a question forms the starting point for design explorations. We want to learn to trust our heart's desire to give us the strength to withstand what confronts designers at the start of every project—the unknown.

EXERCISE: FINDING YOUR HEART'S DESIRE

In pairs, divide into a designer and a listener. The role of the designer is to describe, declare, and speculate about every aspect of a current project, without any interruption or comment, in as much detail as possible. The emphasis is on the complete freedom of the designer to express his or her sense of the design. The listener's job is to take notes. What is important is to really listen without judgment and be as patient as you can. Give the designer all the attention!

When the designer is completely finished, the listener then reports back to the designer the key ideas and images that have been stated. It's important to let the designer know what elements were repeated and where there was particular emphasis, concentration, and clarity, as well as what is not clear. The listener reflects back not only the ideas, but also the energy of the ideas.

The goal of this exercise is to have the experience of the project confirmed by its author. If the project does not sound quite right to its author, then the designer must clarify his or her ideas again. When the listener reads back the text of the design desires, it is useful to read it carefully, circling all the metaphors and poetic phrases. Each of these can be followed up with a drawing, collage, or model. Every described condition and setting needs to be drawn after the exercise is over. The next goal of the exercise is to see if all the ideas can be condensed into a concentrated and vibrant seed that will grow the project. Usually the listener will be able to articulate the essence of the project, a repeated phrase or a sensual condition that may not have been obvious to the designer. This note needs to be sounded back to the designer for reflection.

The listener may seem to have the less glamorous job in this exercise, but I always see the listener as the container and enabler of the entire experience, the one who really holds the experience together. This type of exchange, when done by students of design, approximates the dialogue that goes on inside the mind of an experienced designer. But even with experienced designers, articulating design intentions is liberating and empowering. In my experience, once the exercise has begun, it generates tremendous energy.

At the start of a complicated architectural project, I gave this exercise out to about 20 students and then left the room. A few minutes later I returned to find the room vibrating with energy, as passionate young designers described in rich detail projects that were a few minutes old. I noticed that the temperature in the room had risen—the hearts' desires were burning up the place.

EXERCISE: WHAT DO YOU LIKE?

I have always been attracted to traditional Japanese objects because of the way they balance amenity and materiality and express their making. What about this is so important? They help me bring this state of appreciation of materiality and natural process into the world. They are exemplary without being demanding. I feel a physical sense of satisfaction, as if I have been nourished by a well-conceived, well-cooked meal. A part of myself that I didn't realize was hungry is fulfilled by this nourishment. It lets me grow and include aspects of myself that would otherwise be excluded.

The purpose of the following exercises is to become more familiar with what moves you. You will get to know who you are through what you like.

1. Make of list of your favorite things. Visualize them or bring some of them together. Arrange them in some form of composition. Everything we choose has a meaning. What do these things have in common? Ask yourself why you like them? What are their design qualities? What do they have to say to you? Go through each room in your house and reflect on the space and its artifacts. You can even look at your city in the same way.

2. Use your imagination to visualize something that would make you happy. Something that would make your family or community happy. Something that would make your town or city happy.

3. Think of the place where you spend most of your time. Are you at home there? If so, why? What makes that place feel "right"? If it doesn't, why not?

Starting a project by connecting to your heart's desire generates the creative power necessary to survive the resistance, constraints, and hardship that inevitably accompany the transformation of an idea into matter. The complexity, doubt, and difficulty that naturally occur in the planning, managing, and construction of something will overwhelm a project that does not have a heartfelt essence at its core. Projects that have this heartfelt essence inspire people. At the same time, with this starting point, the designer must guard him or herself against the arrogance and sense of power that can easily seduce us and spoil our creativity.

As a designer recognizes the sensation of being moved, a new phase of development begins. Anyone can be open and therefore moved, but for designers this moment has even greater significance and responsibility; it is the precise moment when the possibility of transformation comes alive. The designer's new responsibility at this point is to investigate exactly what has moved him or her and why.

This is an important discipline for designers—it teaches us about ourselves, about how to embed these inspirations in our own work so that they can be imparted to others.

After three years of studying architecture in London, I arranged to meet an old friend in Union Station in Toronto. Though we had not spoken in several months, I was looking forward to catching up with him because we had always been moved by similar things. I arrived early and stood in the great hall of the railway terminal as the sun poured through the west window. The light took my eyes up into the enormous vaulted space where the names of every stop of the Transcanada train were cut into the stone cornice. That very moment, a heavy nasal voice began to echo over the public address system, announcing the Transcanada's arrival. "Vancouver, Calgary, Regina, Saskatoon, Winnipeg, Thunder Bay, Toronto." I followed the itinerary by reading along the cornice as though the names of the cities were the words of a prayer. Something inside me went still and I fell into a trance, hypnotized by history and the cadence in the conductor's garbled announcement. Meanwhile, all around me, commuters ran for seats on the subway and local trains that now dominate traffic through Union Station. This place is a great anchor and gateway in the life of the city. It is the city's vestibule. When I was young I used to wander though the building at night. I once found an unlocked stair and made my way into the attic and discovered a space that was being used by the railway employees as a shooting range. An unobstructed span, hundreds of feet long, formed in the wooden trusses of the roof. There is simply no other space like it in the city.

When my friend arrived, we were both inspired by the great space, but what had changed was my newfound desire to investigate why I felt so moved and how the built world had moved me. I wanted to know why and how a space could inspire the drawings and notes I made in my journal. I began to observe what was happening inside me, wanting to track as many of the signals and causal connections that link our inner and outer worlds as I could. I began to reflect on the power of built things to move us.

We can learn about ourselves by watching what happens to us when we are moved. It can be as simple as becoming aware of being moved in response to sense impressions. When we are open to something we can learn to watch the act of receiving and allow it to naturally shift into feeling. Becoming mindful of the many different "yes" and "no" moments–and perhaps even the "I don't know" moments–that accompany us throughout our experience of the world offers the designer a rich inventory of inner design experience. For a designer, this is where "knowing" comes from. While some would argue that the world is too busy for these subtle levels of sensitivity, the advertising industry has long understood them and played with their power. We have to fortify our capacity to be sensitive in the world, as it exists and as we have made it, so that we can learn from the reality of our responses. Our job is to sustain awareness in the act of being moved across as many sensing vehicles as possible. We want to allow ourselves to register the impressions of the world in ourselves and let the expressions of ourselves be represented in the world. This dual movement gives us a tangible connection between the world and the psyche.

This inner/outer connection points to the value of getting to know what moves us: it strengthens our capacity to express the same in our built work. Bringing our feelings to what we design can seem daunting, but we expect the same in musicians and writers. We are willing to work at adapting new approaches when it comes to technology–why not the same with bringing our feelings into design?

At the end of a term, I asked a group of architecture students to name the project that most inspired them, and the range was predictably wide. The works were drawn from every possible culture and every possible time period. Naturally, each person will be moved by something different. Yet when I asked them to tell me how these diverse projects made them feel, what the inspiration felt like, their responses were very similar. Not only is the experience of being moved universal, but the actual sensation is very similar from person to person. We all search–and probably hope–for a connection with the feeling of being moved because the resulting ecstasy and, certainly, joy feeds our souls. Designers who recognize this in themselves have the greatest opportunity to bring this quality into the built world. Being moved not only gives us material to experience and analyze internally, it also gives us the energy that makes a creative breakthrough possible.

Insight

Once we are open to receiving, we can begin to notice when we are moved. If we are willing to watch this process—not judge it, but accept, investigate, analyze, and pay attention to it—insight has a chance to naturally arise. Insight reveals the essence of something; it tells us that our search for the truth has been sincere. Insight is the outcome of a process and because it belongs to a process, it is impossible to manufacture without the necessary experience of being open and moved.

Insight is like a sudden condensation. It often feels as though it comes suddenly, unexpectedly, with a silent *plop!* when many subtle conditions are in place. An insight can arrive early in a process, but, in my experience, it more usually arrives after long, often tedious, searching that can sometimes be quite grinding. It may come as an image, an answer to a veiled question, a dream, or a single word. It has a feeling of certainty, but not arrogance. Being open allows us to be moved and this movement indicates we have received something—insight is knowing at the root level of experience.

Insight means seeing into it..."in-tu-it." See in to it. Knowing taken to its essence.

My favorite experience as a teacher is helping others to recognize their own insights—it's quite common in the beginning for students not to be able to do it alone. I often think this is because an insight can be a surprisingly ordinary thing and we would prefer something more spectacular or dramatic. Sometimes this is because we want to see the entire image all at once. But insight can be about a single step, perhaps just a glimmer in the distance, and so it sometimes takes another person to point it out.

Another way to recognize if your insight is closer than you think is to see if there is something you have been returning to again and again. It might be something right in front of you, like a guest who is already inside your home while you are still watching at the window. Insight may exist in a drawing that has a certain charisma to it or in a simple phrase that illuminates things afresh. It's a very delicate moment. All you need is to take one step into the new idea, to open the door just wide enough for a glimpse.

The power of a glimpse can be best explained by a simple exercise. If you look out the window for a few seconds and take in the scene, you will find you can occupy yourself for 10 minutes describing all that you have seen. The same is true for an insight. The glance may only last a second, during which time the eye takes in an immense amount of information. The verbal or written or drawn description of that same scene to another may take much longer. An insight can carry design work a great distance.

To experience insight is to see with ease into the nature of what is happening. Insight cannot be forced. It arises because earlier conditions have been satisfied and we are, for a moment, at one with the object. Although the insight may feel sudden, remember that it rests first on being open, and then on being moved, which means that a great amount of conscious and unconscious work has been done. There is no obstruction in the form of judgment or opinion. Insight contains the answer to a question that has been focusing our attention. A really good question or intention is the most valuable thing to carry with us and guide us through the creative journey. Insight is the inner dimension of being moved, and it refreshes the energy we require to travel through the iterative journey of design.

There are two levels at work here: insight into something we observe in the world and insight into something we observe inwardly. There is an "otherness" to insight because, like the "Aha!" that comes from a dream understood, insight comes from another point of view. Its source is beyond our ego-centered take on the world. An insight satisfies our appetite for the truth about things. Deep inside ourselves we understand that we are experiencing true and authentic learning. Insight may be the product of a long or short process, but the moment always feels like a revelation. The suddenness of intuition can feel like a micro-shock to our belief system. The traditional understanding of this is that the new seeing may come from a distant part of ourselves, perhaps from a higher self. It can't be forced, but once experienced, the energy it produces washes through us. It has a quality that realigns and recalibrates the way we approach a particular project or, indeed, the world. As exciting and fulfilling as this may be, it is in no way a completion–but it has increased the chances that we will be able to understand more fully.

When an insight is born, we experience a feeling of pure knowing, a feeling of receiving something total or whole. Even if an insight contradicts what we want to believe, it is fulfilling. It helps us remember that the death of something always marks the birth of something else. After an insight, we experience an unmistakable feeling of gratitude. In a way, this sense of gratitude is a good test of whether our insight is genuine. Insight not only relieves a certain pressure during the creative process, it also leaves us with a more open heart.

A Unit of Design: A Question Answered

Insight and the act of design are deeply linked because it is the nature of design to organize, prioritize, and unify disparate phenomena. I found myself asking, How do you know if you have actually accomplished something when you begin to design? What is the measure you can use to judge? When we travel by car or bike we can keep track of our progress by figuring out how far we travel in a hour. How do designers measure their progress? How do we give the creative mind suggestions without giving it instructions that limit creativity? I have found that every creative search inherently rests on a question, whether it is asked consciously or unconsciously. For me, therefore, the smallest unit of design is simply a question answered.

I began experimenting with this approach by listening to the experience of students as they described their work. I began to watch the busy inner flow of my own creative thoughts and images that accompanied the search for design solutions. I explored this creative stream from different angles until I could slow down my inner environment.

Let's look at this process more closely. When we are designing we are usually trying different approaches and configurations. We are carrying on an internal dialogue and answering our own questions through the creation of images, text, or drawings. What happens if I move that over here? Would it be better if the top of the building were shaped like this? Is that window really in the best place? I don't like that. I like this. There is a constant stream of inner commentary that accompanies our creations–a great deal of it silent and unconscious. What is important is that after a few years of studying design, we become increasingly aware that this is going on and learn how to participate in it consciously. The tone and immediacy of this voice becomes our companion in the creative world. By slowing down and reflecting on this process, I want to examine what happens when we become more aware of it. Can we actually use our awareness of this process to enhance our creative search?

The inner world of design is activated by a call and response–a question asked and answered. I imagine it as the kind of interaction heard in religious services when the leader calls out a question and the congregation answers in unison. Following a designer's question (call), the response is received in the form of an image or impulse from the unconscious. I think of this dynamic that occurs during the design process as the "designers' liturgy." It is at the center of the sacred studio and is the designer's inner instrument of creation. The call is an ascending appeal and the response is a descent of that appeal into matter. Like inhaling and exhaling, the two are complementary and form a natural creative cycle. They need each other to complete the cycle of design, a cycle of question and response that is naturally iterative and reflects the fact that an experiment is taking place. We never know the outcome when we start out on a creative task because the outcome, by definition, is unknown. As a byproduct of making the built world, designers learn to unconsciously explore the inner world of images, rituals, and unrecognized instincts that accompany and enable the transformation of spirit into matter.

What is happening inside the designer's mind during the process of design? When we set out to design something, we bring two worlds together. The world we are conscious of includes the conditions of the building site, the client's needs, and the budget

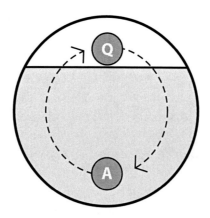

A UNIT OF DESIGN
A Question Answered

challenges, as well as complex issues concerning function, amenity, and building technology. The other world that needs to come into play involves our ability to relate to the unconscious world. All the facts of the project do not make a design—if design were an activity guided only by rational thought, we would not have thousands of different teapots, chairs, trucks, sailboats, and houses. In practice, both rational and irrational urges guide the designer. The challenge of design is to resolve the problem that is not usually declared or explicit. The client may ask for a house, hotel, or airport, but there is always a problem inside the overt question: What exactly is a house, hotel, or airport in the context we are working with? This underlying problem can only be discovered through the process of design, the process of searching for something that we know is there, but is temporarily out of sight.

Intention

If you want your creativity to be helpful to others you need to make this intention conscious. Before you start your work, become conscious of your own articulation of the quest you are embarking on. This can begin with a simple ritual that allows you ask questions like "Why am I doing this?" "Who am I doing this for?" There are obviously many layers involved in answering such questions and your responsibility is to find out what level you are addressing when you undertake your work. Many people unconsciously address the intention of their project by having a photograph of someone they admire or a project they admire near their desk. Defining the intention of your project is like describing the door you will go through during the design process. The door may be large or small, humble or grand. It may be a door that has meaning only for you or it may matter to a very large community. Similarly, you can "close" a design session by giving thanks for what you have received. The important thing is that you make an effort to be conscious of what you are doing and that you not get caught in blaming others for the status of your work.

The Question

The questions we ask are perhaps the most underrated aspect of the design process. They are underrated because so much of what prompts our design decisions are unconscious questions inherent in the creative process. To some extent, design is simply the answer to a question we are not really aware we are asking. The process of design is driven by making the questions conscious–some through drawings and others as the result of reflection and visualizing possibilities before creating images.

The purpose of the question is to bring the mind into the process. I am not talking about negative or obsessive thinking, but the creative and constructive activity of the mind that is brilliantly capable of investigating through analysis and serious questioning. This positive, questioning mind is an aspect of the ego that drives the project forward like a motor, prompting, containing, and grounding the unconscious. The question is the spark that ignites creativity. It is sent into the unknown and we watch for what tumbles from the place of unknowing onto the page before us.

Some Useful Questions
What's it like?
Does this help? If not, what would help?
Is this what I want?
What helps me to feel good about this project?

41

Is it soulful?
Is it related to my inspiration?
What do I like most about the idea?
This project needs more_____?
This project needs less_____?

What are the questions you are aware of asking as you design? What questions would you add to this list?

The question is also the rudder of our creative process—we will go in the direction set by it. To do this effectively, we need to address still another layer of the question: the emotional tone we establish inwardly when asking it. This is particularly essential when you consider that we often don't ask a question consciously. We begin to sketch or draw as though the images were coming from somewhere else rather than from ourselves—albeit unconsciously. Including your heart's desire in the formation of a question will help to ensure that the emotional tone of the question is positive and true. The simplest way to accomplish this is to take a moment to ask yourself about what you want—before addressing the project. When we consciously ask a question, we are committing to owning our intentions during the process of design.

The question is an active ingredient. It's job is to prompt or activate the unconscious. The question is a message sent from the conscious mind to the unconscious mind. The whole premise of design starts with an aspiration to produce something new. An original design presumes there is something unknown to be discovered. This unknown will come into being through the way you move through the creative process. If our question is too rigid, or too narrow, or too far from the present, then we will likely get back an answer that doesn't help us. This is because we are resigning ourselves to a very limited relationship with the unknown. The psyche is no more responsive to a flagrant act of will than to extreme dullness. In order to establish a relationship with the unknown, the question must be genuine. It will then fly into the unknown—powered not by will but by the heart's desire for an answer—and lift our heart's desire into the unknown.

The purpose of the question is to illuminate. The first question sends up sparks. It is a request for material, for images. What is it like? What is it about? The naming of an architectural place or element. The request for a detail, a section, a material. The role of the question varies with its nature–a precise question challenges the creative faculty differently from a general one. Asking about the color of the front door is very different from asking what it feels like to stand in front of the door. When the creative mind is allowed to expand we can access a greater depth and range of possibilities. A more focused question is no less valuable, but by asking it we are, to a greater degree, self-selecting the answer.

The influence of the question can be subtle: every nuance generates something. It always includes facets that are not detected by the conscious mind but may have implications from the unconscious mind. What makes this dynamic so powerful is the difference between the conscious mind and the unconscious mind. There is a natural charge in these polarities. A question that may seem insignificant to the conscious mind can have great reverberations in the unconscious mind. Likewise an image generated by an unconscious fantasy may set off fireworks in the conscious mind.

The Gap

After a question has been asked, there is a moment when we feel as though we have lost contact with the world. Like a ship losing sight of the shore, we send our question out into the unknown. This delicate moment actually has the affect of arousing our awareness in the same way that trying to spot something in the distance increases our concentration. We squint. We change our perspective. What I often find most effective is the same thing that I find most difficult: to let go of my expectations and try to let things happen inwardly. To surrender, relax, and bring patience and faith to the journey is not just good advice–these states of mind have been scientifically measured through neurological testing to be helpful in creative problem solving. An image may come in the blink of an eye, but the gap in time may stretch to anxious minutes, hours, weeks, or even years. This is a heightened time when awareness of the moment is all there is. We are waiting for something to happen, alert but not in charge. We are waiting for the unconscious to speak to us. We are not stuck, but we need to remember that we are not in control. If no answer comes, and we are impatient, one approach is to draw an earlier idea, or recycle something from memory. Another is simply to ask another question. But if no response comes at all, there is a good chance that the question needs to be reframed or restated.

Receiving

To be receptive means surrendering to the process and recording what comes. We need to train ourselves to wait patiently as though we were not expecting a thing. At the same time, we need to be ready to record as fully as possibly the signals that return to us—the messages from our own unconscious. If the gap is a moment of emptiness, the process of recording asks us to become as open and receptive and nonjudgmental as possible. This is the opposite of using muscles; this is using buttery-soft receptors. This is no simple task because the more we strain to receive the less likely we are to receive, yet if we lose interest we will miss the message. This calls for a state of equilibrium that may last for a blink of an eye or for minutes, perhaps hours, at a time.

A good way to practice this is to spend extended periods of time listening to a friend or a child. Ask them a question and then listen attentively and observe them patiently. When you feel yourself losing interest, extend the practice; see if you can deepen your attention. The more full and complete our receptivity, the more we can receive messages from our own imagination and the more we will be given. It is as though the unconscious knows the strength of the container. It will not give an image if that image will be ignored. It is meeting the question halfway in the place where psyche and matter touch—spirit coming into matter. This interior liturgy is a key piece of the design process. When the inner studio is awake, we are practicing with awareness.

When the raw material has been contacted and there is an image to work with, the next level in the process involves a similar dynamic but makes a subtle shift in emphasis toward the world of matter. In the early stages the elaboration and shaping of the products of the unconscious took precedence. We now need to go into something concrete and material. We are no longer searching for the image, but working with it, and a different set of skills needs to come into play: shaping, forming, coloring, fabricating.

Do it again and again

A question answered forms a single unit of design. Stringing together several units of design in testing the results is called the iterative process. I like to imagine that with every unit of design completed the project experiences a birthday. A project that has answered one question may well seem precocious, but a project that has been through hundreds and thousands of questions and answers is going to be wise and creative and have made contact with a deeper kind of beauty. To paraphrase the American poet Charles Olsen, every perception must be followed by another perception.

This is a crucial stage and many projects collapse under the weight of questions that becomes to critical or harsh. Keep in mind that first glimpses are fragile. A general rule of thumb is to rule out nothing and to remain curious, patient, and playful. Let your questions be sincere and make them count.

As this energy subsides, the key is to remember that our work is not done; it is just beginning. This is the moment when a new idea is putting its first roots into the conscious world. We need to cultivate these new tendrils. We need make sure the next question is based on what moves us. If we connect immediately to the image, then a new cycle of question and response begins based on this. Questions beget images and those images inspire new questions. We are generating units of design. We are sustaining the creative energy of the project. If the image is not right or there is no connection with the process, then we need to go back to our original question—which is to say we go back to our heart's desire and ask, "What about this project matters most to us?"

Into the feeling of process

Animate, illuminate, contain—gather and harvest. All of this can happen in no time when a question is answered. The call-and-response of the designer's liturgy asks us to become aware of our inner world and creatively manage the tension of these opposites until we feel in our hearts and minds that something right has come into being. Learning when to lead and when to follow during the creative process is a subtle art in itself.

The crux of this process is to become aware of the energetic difference between seeking and receiving, and learning to be attentive to the needs of each pulsation. They are opposites, but that does not make them enemies; in fact, they are intimately linked in the creative dance. The more complex and interesting experience is the actual process of working with these two different pulsations. Too much questioning and there is nothing to receive; too much reception and nothing is generated. It's an inner balancing act in which the designer wants to be squarely in the middle. Some people enjoy one aspect more than the other, but the purpose of trying to make the process more conscious is to allow for some balance so the less-developed aspect can be cultivated.

It doesn't really matter if the process is moving from spirit into matter or matter into spirit. The starting point is less significant than the relationship that these two opposites are able to briefly have, like a moment of weightlessness as the two aspects become perfectly equal. Our job as designers is to support their equality. We are trying to become the most natural environment for creating an original creative thought. We want to become, within ourselves, the best possible setting for fantasy and imagination. All of this starts inwardly, with getting to know the difference between the feeling of the activation and the feeling of receptivity. At its foundation the creative principle is a union of opposites. Learning when to lead and when to follow is all part of the dance in the inner studio.

UNIT OF DESIGN EXERCISE:
GROUP QUESTIONS AND ANSWERS

This exercise is intended to activate otherwise unseen possibilities inside a design project. It is done in pairs at the start of the project: one person is the listener and one is the designer.

Step 1

The listener has six questions to ask. Questions of clarification are possible, but listening is the key. Pay attention to what the designer is saying. Listen for phrases, poetic descriptions, juxtapositions, and imagery that have an enlivened, energetic quality.

The six questions are:

What do you hope for?

Who is it for?

What is it?

What happens there?

How would you like it to be remembered?

The designer is free to play with description—there is no need to be too serious; it is better to be playful and simple.

When the designer has answered all the questions (allow 25–30 minutes) the listener synthesizes the response into key images, symbols, poetic metaphors, or symbolic activities. These are presented back to the designer impartially for reflection. The dialogue that follows seeks a consensus of key images that the designer and listener agree sums up the work.

Step 2

The listener uses a dream or symbol dictionary and reads the meaning of the key image or symbol to the designer. The designer then brings this image into the active imagination practice for developing the project.

Taking Care of your Ideas

Teaching design, I've noticed that students often produce interesting images and then immediately become stuck. They simply do not know what to do with their inspiration. They do not know how to love an idea through the act of design. They do not know how to take care of their baby. Like a first glimpse, a first idea is fragile and will not stand severe criticism. The author must nurture his or her own work carefully. I have found myself saying to students, "If I worked for you and you asked me to develop a design based on this image, I would have more then enough to develop this project." One inspired image is enough to begin and, once started, the discipline of the design process can move the project through to completion.

Understanding

If we are open, we will be moved, and if we are moved and investigate this feeling, we have the chance to get insight and the great test of insight is that it results in understanding.

The meaning of "understanding" is contained in the word itself: it is about seeing something from below, from a more humble, less power-centered vantage point, where one's previously held positions and opinions are less involved in the act of perception. Insight is an enabling force; it seems to arrive with a sudden surge. But understanding is empowering because it directs the higher seeing of insight directly into the thick tangle of matter. The patience required to await insight deepens to an acceptance as understanding works its way through experience, unraveling a problem in the material world. We are closer to the way material behaves, and this means things move more slowly. We are stepping more directly into the process, with less velocity and more centeredness. We are in a more deliberate and conscious mood, working through implications, ramifications, and adjustments.

This phase of work has us directly testing our speculations. The pieces may have to be taken apart and fitted together again differently, but insight always brings enough energy to rework a previous understanding. We are being moved, but this time we have insight to guide us, and understanding to empower us to act. We really can't go backward once we begin to process and apply an insight. We are moving material through to a resolution, working past old programming and preparing material to hold the new insight.

Students often collect data, analyze it, come up with important insights–and then they get stuck. Why would one get stuck after so much accomplishment? I think that this happens because the energy that produced the insight has to shift. How can we help our insight become understanding? The test of insight ("Does it produce understanding?") demands patience, resolve, and determination of us. Insight comes upon us suddenly, while understanding comes more slowly. Insight arrives with a kind of velocity, and needs to be treated as something precious. You have a chance to actually learn something from your insight. Before it arrives, you have never met it before; you have been waiting for its arrival, nonetheless it is a surprise. How can you learn about the insight? Try exploring a relationship with it. Treat it like a newfound friend. Ask it questions about itself. Ask yourself questions about it. What are its implications? Another insight may arise, and then, through the answer, understanding arises. Understanding involves us in patiently or steadfastly listening, assimilating, and digesting. Insight without understanding will leave us stuck and our work will seem not fully formed.

Understanding makes us feel whole and happy. When we understand something, others naturally recognize this and often are drawn to ask about it. We don't have to force the understanding on others; they will naturally be attracted to its contents. So another characteristic of understanding is that it benefits many people–it is naturally harmonizing. The door of understanding, once open to us, is naturally there for others to experience through the way it is embodied in our work. Understanding brings an exemplary quality to our design work. It is a kind of beauty that lingers like a deep porch overlooking a garden.

Stabilizing the idea

A key moment in the life of any creative project occurs very early in its development. This is the moment immediately after the design is born, when the designer needs to begin developing his or her project. Remember that inspiration is something we receive– once we have received it, we need to become aware of the qualities that distinguish our work so that we can consciously develop them. At this stage of work we begin the tricky process of balancing inflation and humility, in which the authors must learn to both separate from and have affection for their designs. Becoming aware of the essence of your idea and analyzing its qualities is really the introduction of the ego into the creative process. Without this step we may never be able to develop the richness and complexity of our projects. Stabilizing the design involves the active acceptance of constraints and problems without losing the vibrant creative core of the idea.

Take heart from the fact that every great work of fiction or poetry was written without the author needing to add to the twenty-six letters of the alphabet. Your project most likely already has all the basic ingredients that are necessary for it to evolve. A relatively finite number of timeless architectural elements are at your disposable to be arranged in an infinite number of ways: shelter, ritual, materiality, setting, and sustainability. Identify and use the idea that has inspired you. There is usually less need to generate new ideas and more need to analyze the fundamental idea and nurture it. Stabilizing the idea means consciously developing and refining the language that will convey what you want the project to say and do. To accomplish this, you need to understand the hierarchy of elements inherent in your idea and concentrate your time on what is most significant.

At this stage I often see projects lose their way. A great idea becomes lost among a dozen other ideas competing for attention. The big conceptual thrust of the work is undone by smaller less convincing decisions. It is as though the authors of the work do not really accept the potential of their ideas, so they unconsciously start the creative process all over again, blindly developing new ideas, with each iteration becoming less and less meaningful.

In the beginning it is far easier to stabilize a design by having someone listen to you describe your work, perhaps even letting them draw what they hear you saying, than it is by trying to recognize it yourself. Even if the person listening to your idea offers very little feedback, as long as the listening is genuine, you will find that your idea takes hold and begins to grow.

With experience our creative instincts become clearer and more resilient. The inner studio is the place where we can practice tuning into our creative instincts and learn to trust their call.

PART THREE

Inner Resources

Anything can be a creative resource—any circumstance, physical symptom, dream, or emotional state. This is possible simply because what makes something a resource is not what it is, or whether we like it, but our relationship to it. When we become conscious of what we are experiencing we have the potential to learn from it. For example, when you get angry because you are stuck on a project, there is nothing you can do about your circumstances. When you feel angry you are literally absorbed in your anger. You have no choice about the state you are in. You can't possibly make any good use of your anger and it probably won't actually help you free yourself. But if you become aware of your anger, everything changes. The moment you are aware of your anger, you are no longer absorbed by it. The part of you that observes the anger is actually quite peaceful, which helps break the spell and makes that energy available for something more useful to you—like getting a new idea. Also when you become aware of being angry, you can make a decision about whether to stay angry.

None of this is possible without awareness. Awareness gives you a chance to make a decision about what is best for you and the people around you. This powerful way of seeing combines observation, non-judgment, and affection. Awareness is an important experience in the creative process because it automatically unifies body, mind, and emotions.

Experts in neuroscience, biology, physics, and healing all agree that the mind and body are best approached as a single entity. Seeing the mind and body as inseparable not only opens the door to understanding the new role our physical bodies can play in the experience of awareness, but brings our minds and bodies onto equal footing. Awareness is neither thinking alone nor feeling alone, but a synthesis that brings both mind and body into a single knowing voice that can guide decision making and problem solving. This knowing voice is the basis for creativity and wisdom and is completely portable—equally at home with any circumstance we may face. The purpose of awareness is to put us directly in touch with the unified response of our minds and bodies.

We have all heard the advice that we need to "listen" to ourselves. But what exactly does that mean—and how do we learn to do it effectively? What part of ourselves are we supposed to listen to? Do I listen to the messages of my body or my mind? How do I learn to read the signals and interpret these messages? How do I turn inner resources into creativity and wisdom?

Again, awareness is the key. Like any skill, awareness can be learned and improved upon with practice, and comes to us with many years of testing already performed. Meditation is the traditional practice for training ourselves to develop awareness, but anything we do repeatedly has the potential to serve as a meditation. I always see the creative process as having the potential to be an object of meditation. But the greatest benefit of awareness is that it allows you to do something about your own circumstances. It allows you to use your own circumstances to grow and turn anything into a creative resource. In this section, I want to look at body, dreams, and psychological shadow as resources that can become the sources of creativity and wisdom when we bring awareness to the act of design.

Our ability to connect to the symptoms, messages, and signals of our bodies, dreams, and shadow offers us three doors to the unconscious. Each has its own unique voice and each offers us the opportunity to bring to the built world a wise part of ourselves that is often ignored. Body, dream, and shadow are with us all the time. This chapter is not only concerned with developing our ability to listen to "inner messages" about design, but with the very real possibility of designing spaces and artifacts that support these explorations for others. My hope is that we are able to bring more of the richness of the inner world to the built world by bringing these dimensions of the psyche into our work. The reality of the unconscious has been a cornerstone of Western psychology, but the actual capacity to make the unconscious conscious as a reality of the built world rests with designers who have the experience and the skills to work with introspection and the inner world of the psyche.

The inner studio is home to the creative world that lives inside us and asks to be built, represented, and acknowledged in the places and artifacts of the built world. What keeps the designer on the level and willing to inwardly negotiate through the intense enthusiasms of the design process? Listening to his or her own body, dreams, and shadow. These aspects of the psyche all support transformation and are constantly sending messages that will guide us and help create a sense of direction and traction through design difficulties. The sign of their inclusion is a relaxed attitude, an inner knowing that allows us to enjoy our work in spite of all the risks involved. The inner studio is resource-rich, a container where spirit and matter are brought together until they become one with our hearts' desires. We are searching for a way to generate images that not only matter deeply to us and make us happy, but have the greatest opportunity for bringing the same to the built world.

The Body

Too much animal distorts the civilized man, too much civilization makes sick animals.
–C.G. JUNG

The Body as Designer

My own experience about the wisdom and creativity of the body had a very simple starting point. I had just recovered from the flu and found myself without any energy. Whenever I tried to return to a busy life, flu-like symptoms would return and I would need to rest; then the debilitating cycle of symptoms would repeat itself. I became increasingly worried and afraid that I would never recover my strength. This went on for weeks, then months, and then years. I saw specialists and was sent for a series of medical tests looking for tumors, parasites, depression, and blood-related problems. Nothing showed up. I tried a wide range of alternative body and mind treatments, and while some of these lifted my spirits, the chronic weakness always returned. Finally, out of desperation and with nothing to lose, I decided to simply pay closer attention to whatever made me feel stronger or weaker. At first, I couldn't really discern or trust the feedback I was getting from my body, but eventually I began to discover that when I was completely honest with myself, I felt stronger. It was a subtle sensation, but I felt I had found a path. The truth not only brought me mental and emotional wellbeing, it also translated into increased physical energy.

This was a turning point in my life. I grew closer to my body by paying attention to the way it responded to phone calls, circumstances, places, and people. If I was going to have the immune system of an orchid, I might as well try to learn from it. I began to appreciate the wisdom and creativity of my body. And I also had to admit I had learned something from my affliction.

In the beginning, when I received an invitation to an event I thought I very much wanted or needed to attend, I would check in with my body to read the signals before accepting or rejecting it. These signals often took the form of symptoms. I found myself involved in a non-stop process of taking a personal energy inventory of circumstances and opportunities. Everything had to wait, and as more and more things waited, some just dropped away, and new activities took hold. It took years for me to stop arguing with my body's symptoms, more time to hear the voice behind the symptoms, and then more patience to accept the wisdom of the messages. Looking back at the process, I realize that I was like a student learning a new language. By the time I had recovered enough energy to re-enter the world, I found myself in an entirely new relationship to my body, with a new set of desires and ambitions. Any setbacks I have experienced since then have always led to insights that deepened my understanding of the contribution the body makes to our happiness in the world.

As designers we typically associate creativity, intuition, and imagination exclusively with the mind, yet architecture has traditionally been built largely by hand, and is responsible for sheltering and affecting the whole person. Indeed, one goal of any successful architectural project, beyond its capacity to support practical and safe functioning, is to satisfy needs that are less easily expressed, such as comfort and an emotional sense of belonging–perhaps even the capacity to inspire hope and creativity. It seems natural to bring our bodies' innate capacity to create and express to the design process because it is the body, with its extraordinary sense and range of touch, that we are actually seeking to contact and satisfy.

Embedded in the way society now lives is a set of beliefs that strongly impacts architectural design, a set of beliefs that overvalues thinking and underestimates the potential of the body to invoke imagination, arouse decision making, and guide the creative process. Modern life involves us in machine-like living. Our dependence on pervasive mechanical and automated systems turns all natural systems, including our bodies, into a liability. Unlike machines, however, our bodies will not always perform according to our wishes or keep up with all that we hope to accomplish. Instead of rejecting what our bodies are trying to tell us because they are prone to fatigue, sickness, and bouts of unreliability, we need to become conscious of our vulnerabilities so they can be included in the world. Precisely because our bodies are imperfect, they offer a unique perspective for understanding the relationship between the built world and ourselves.

In fact, our bodies provide places that our emotions and souls can call home, and the range of feelings that we experience through the body not only civilizes, but ultimately and fundamentally humanizes, the way we live, work, and think.

Psychologically speaking, the body is associated with the unconscious because in our daily lives we are simply not conscious of its functioning or its wisdom. The way my eyes actually process visual data, the way my spleen regulates sugar levels, the way my digestive system processes food–these complex operations take place below the threshold of awareness. Our sense of sight does not require conscious involvement. I have never been involved in supervising the functioning of my glandular system or the electrical pulsations that become thoughts or movements. There is an innate, instinctive intelligence at work on our behalf. We usually only notice the body when it has a complaint; otherwise, we are happy to not center ourselves there because to do so would compromise our intellectually oriented habits and ambitions. We do whatever we can to superficially keep it happy or override its attempt to contact us. Yet to ignore it leaves us split, with a belief structure that identifies the body with the Third World and the mind with the modern First World.

The body has been evolving for as long as consciousness itself; it is full of creativity, intelligence, and wisdom and is capable of not only following the orders we give it, but of sending us important signals. Thinking, or intellect, is also vital to creativity, but is not sufficient because it ignores much of who we are.

This mind/body imbalance is a hallmark of modern life and is visible around us. At the same time, some great buildings or great places touch us deeply and stir unknown parts of ourselves. Why is this? It's because they reach us on more than one level. Their power to move us comes from their ability to include more of the rich and complex levels that we unconsciously know ourselves to be. This concept of ourselves as composed of a more complex anatomy is supported by advances in psycho-immunology that describe human beings as containing a physical body, an emotional body, and a mental body all working in concert. The speed of our lives and our habitual patterns of perception lead us to view these distinct aspects of the self from a narrow, fragmented perspective. Sometimes we need refuge from the weather, but we may also need an environment that can provide a refuge for our nervous systems or a place where our minds are free to roam.

When we relax, it's natural to make contact with the different qualities of each of these three bodies. Looking back on a day, it is possible to see moments that have been very physical, other moments that were plainly emotional, and other times that were given over to thinking or reflection. All of these different parts of the self appear to have been mysteriously and seamlessly invoked and managed. We take for granted that when a part of us is leading, the other parts of us conveniently agree to follow. It's helpful to understand our bodies as having different qualities. The physical body is obviously denser and more centered in matter than, say, the emotional body. The mental seems less constrained by matter and is more receptive to ideas. Each body has an expertise, yet each also has the ability to infiltrate the other, sharing and shaping common or overlapping input. Again, the creative life involves knowing when to lead and when to follow from among these different ways of experiencing the world.

The greater the alignment, cooperation, or communication among the three bodies, the greater our access to their collective resources. The way we work through a creative problem will draw upon the habits we have developed in relation to these three bodies. If one dominates excessively, we are going to be making environments that reflect that bias. A modern approach to design not only involves utilizing new materials and technology, it incorporates our potential for awareness in integrating our bodies' wisdom and creativity into the design process.

Knowing Kinesthetically

The most basic level on which we find our bodies broadcasting their wisdom is through physical symptoms. How can a physical symptom like a headache become a gift? When it allows us to learn something about our relationship to our bodies. We may get angry when physical symptoms arise. We may even start to blame our bodies! Yet our bodies aren't being mean–there isn't an angry bone in anyone's body. We need to use the symptoms that our bodies offer us to learn something about ourselves or we will miss the crucial signals. Headaches often appear to let us know that we have been thinking negatively about ourselves. We may be stuck on false or negative beliefs that compromise our ability to know what direction to go in.

Another symptom that is worth exploring is the common stomach ache. When we feel "tied in knots," or we feel ourselves unable to "stomach" what we are doing, we may have "swallowed" something that we can't "digest." These kinds of complaints often point to us not being true to ourselves. We may have chosen a course of action or made a decision because it pleases an authority figure or our parents. If we become seduced by power and prestige and go against what our gut tells us is best, we will hear from our bodies. An upset stomach may be calling us to review whether we are forcing ourselves to assimilate something that just does not agree with us. Our bodies don't want us to abandon them and are on constant guard to help us through decision making and difficulty. Listening to your body in this way may seem to put you out of step with everyone else, but the chances are great that you will actually find yourself more content with your own life. Every part of the body has a message to deliver. These examples are an invitation for you to examine what parts of your body might have something to say to you as you move through your decision making.

Kinesthetic knowing involves making a shift from a knowing that is centered in the intellect to knowing that is centered in the sensations of the body. The body is clearly able to say yes or no; we have all had the experience of an upset stomach before a stressful event. On a more subtle level, perhaps we have experienced walking into a place for the first time and feeling completely relaxed and at home, whereas someone else may walk into the same room and get a pain in the neck. The body has a great capacity to signal our preferences. The mind can be included through its ability to learn from the responses of the body, its ability to focus into the field of responses that arise in our bodies. When this happens, over time, the body and mind come to decisions that are less split and more unified and the intelligence of the body brings a composite and "earthy" feel to its quality of knowing.

The next time you are walking through a building, down a street, or in a forest, remember that our bodies are always in space and have memories of every kind of space. We need to learn how to listen to bones, flesh, muscles, fascia, and ligaments. "What does my body want?" is a wonderful question for a designer to be in the habit of asking. At first, any of these approaches will need a degree of concentration that feels unnatural. A walk in nature is often the easiest place to begin to apply this awareness, but with practice, the voices of our bodies will be with us all the time.

A very refined example of this ability is dowsing for water. You want to find out where to drill a well, but there are no signs of water on the surface. A dowser comes to the site and walks the land holding a stick in front of him until it begins to vibrate. Many people think that the stick is registering an underground stream or pool of water, but in reality micro-muscular movements of the body in response to the presence of water are amplified through the stick. The body's intelligence can find water, but this communication is too subtle for us to perceive. A subtle or energetic aspect of the body is speaking.

While dowsers may be rare, a first step for most of us might be to accept that there are subtle messages that we are capable of receiving. For example, we know quite spontaneously whether we like or dislike someone or something. To experience this, try walking through an art gallery. Walk slowly, giving yourself permission to gently observe the subtle way your body tightens or relaxes, desires to speed up or linger. Observe your reactions, but try not to pass comment on them. Just allow them to come and go. Changes may occur in response to the people you see, or the images you see, the smells, and the shape of rooms or the air temperature. Let anything be the cause. You may be surprised to discover how constantly we are resonating with and responding with stimuli. Quite simply, we are always being moved. The art is on the wall, but the beauty is often in the sensation we feel when we are moved.

Just as we can point to a physical brain but not to the mind, so we can point to the physical body but not to this more subtle aspect of the body, what is often called the "emotional body, " or the "energetic body." But we can learn to become aware of it and access its rich voice. A benefit of working in this way is that the more we develop awareness, the more, in turn, this promotes the possibility of the built world becoming a place where this aspect of ourselves feels welcome and included. How else are we going to feel that our entire being, the modern self, belongs?

A timeless example that recognizes the existence of the emotional or energetic body is found in the front door to a cathedral. While there is a door to accommodate our physical bodies, it is usually set into a much larger, more important opening that welcomes our emotional or energetic bodies. The energy aspect of our bodies is well known to healers and mystics and was always built into the design of these sacred places. The Great Door at Reims Cathedral features such a door surmounted by a great rose window that recalls the illuminated quality of a chakra.

In many city environments, we find the built world is not worth noticing and only makes an impression on a very narrow portion of our potential awareness. Instinctively, and perhaps unconsciously, we can't agree with the built world. We tune out in a way that, I think, over time, leaves us angry or ready to "zone out" in a bored trance of detachment. The banality of the modern built world is hardly an accident. It is the result of rigorously trained professionals and complex laws. Yet its powerful unconscious beliefs make it incapable of nourishing us in any real way. It exhausts us. We find ourselves overstimulated by the visual and spatial equivalent of refined sugar, while our emotional bodies struggle to find anything nourishing to eat. Our bodies battle to feel acknowledged, while our minds feel overwhelmed by negative messages and codes. The body is actually under attack in some of our modern built environments. The local drug store, where we go for medicine, is an environment devoid of healing. Toxic environments are the direct outcome of a society in which the body is subordinated to the mind. We are not happy in places that refuse to allow our capacity to be whole to thrive. Our society's collective lack of wholeness is unconsciously built into the world.

Listening to Fatigue and Exhaustion

Like the body, the unconscious psyche has an instinctive wisdom that can correct the errors and excesses of consciousness if we are open to its messages.
–E. EDINGER

The way that many of us are introduced to the idea of listening to our bodies is by collapsing from exhaustion and fatigue. Living as we do in the industrial world, it can be difficult to notice the subtle industrialization of human beings that covertly encourages us to think of our bodies as machines. Long periods of uninterrupted creative work or intense multitasking are possible and occasionally necessary, and may even be exhilarating, but it is also extremely demanding on our nervous systems. The truth is that we aren't machines. We have adrenal glands that will not be able to function when we abuse them. From the point of view of our bodies and nervous systems, we have much more in common with natural phenomena than machines. Listening to your body is a powerful antidote to the industrialization of the world and brings insight and understanding to anything you are involved in.

Resting is an art. It is as basic to our wellbeing as eating food. When it comes to eating we learn to choose foods that agree with our sense of taste. We eat what agrees with us and learn to avoid foods that make us feel sick. When it comes to resting, we have a less evolved menu of choices, yet there are as many ways of resting as there are of satisfying our hunger.

A useful first step is to simply ask yourself what your body needs. The next step is to listen without judgment to the answer, which may range from a whisper to a decisive declaration to a cascade of different responses. A friend once admitted he did not want to ask his body what it needed for fear it would tell him to stop working so hard. An early night is different from a siesta. A refreshing conversation with a friend is different from a walk. A stretching routine every morning is different from a long massage. How long has it been since the needs of our bodies or the needs of our creative intelligence were allowed an active voice in our scheduling and design decision making? Do you know of a place or an artifact that refreshes your nervous system? If not, search for such a place or object. If you have already found such places or things, reflect on their power to restore and revive you. These are important experiences to digest.

How do we learn to rest? By listening to our fatigue and exhaustion. This means pausing not just because you may be stuck or lost, but stopping because you are may be mentally tired or you ache physically. Stopping because your body needs to stretch, breathe, move, or rest is as necessary as eating, yet it is surprisingly difficult and undervalued as a creative tool during the design process. The message is very simple: When you feel tired, rest. When you are tired, put the heavy load down. This sounds too simple, yet fatigue and lack of time have become very common obstacles during a creative project. We fail to notice the industrialization of human experience. Exhaustion is a signal that our minds and bodies need refreshment. We are not machines. Our nervous systems are heavily used when we are making creative decisions. Many creative people live in a state of heightened perceptions and the intense use of our senses means we are running the equivalent of a creative marathon when we work intensely. Allowing the psyche a time to rest is an idea as old as the Sabbath.

The key to our difficulty is often found not in a lack of time, but in a lack of respect for our own needs. This habit, if undetected, will be built into the world. We can already see that the busy built world has little regard for nature, the body of the earth. We feel guilty when we put our own needs for health ahead of the task we have been given; we feel we should be able to complete the project without taking a break. We think we should be able to solve every problem. If we pause, we risk losing the respect of some colleague or peer or parent. These notions lead to stress and reflect the shadow that may influence the design process. Exhaustion is like a fire–difficult to extinguish if we wait too long to notice it. Burnout and exhaustion can take years to recover from and seriously impair our decision making. It is much easier to quench our fatigue if we notice its first signals or are prepared to spend some time examining our attitudes and incorporate some healing supports into our approach to design.

I don't mean to suggest that when resting we are no longer creative. My favorite way of creating is to raise questions before I take a rest. Whether I fall asleep or just daydream, I usually find myself with a new sense of direction or fresh creative material when I get back to work. Sometimes we feel physically depleted but our imagination is really quite ready to explore new possibilities–it just doesn't want to be pushed. We are simply expanding the space of creativity to solve the problem of feeling tired. We may need to dream more than to work. We may need to slip into a brief reverie about what we are facing before continuing. I have often thought that Mediterranean cultures hold so many of the Western world's treasures because these cultures practice the afternoon nap or siesta. This enables these cultures to dream twice a day, increasing the chance for the wisdom of the psyche to come through.

Another way of thinking about the creative benefits of relaxing is to understand it as a way of allowing our creative instincts to naturally investigate. When we relax, we are not too focused or attached and can simply enjoy resting in concepts, thoughts, and images as they come and go. Even a moment of this light and playful mind can release tension or lighten our load and refresh our creative options. Relaxing gives problems space, and sometimes space is what enables us to see things in a fresh light. This can be a very lucky time to test other points of view or to see the project through a new lens. With this approach we step back from the project, resting in our imagination. We are amiably experimenting and exploring as we remember to breathe. We want to remain in the creative process but experience expanded horizons.

What if we were asked to design places for discovering refreshment? In the time-starved modern world, simply having the idea of designing a place for resting or relaxing is a good place to start.

EXERCISE

Find a comfortable place to lie down. Loosen any tight clothing, remove your glasses, close your eyes, and breathe naturally. This can often be accomplished by whispering to yourself or saying inwardly something like, "Allow the weight of your body to be totally supported by the floor or mattress. Just let the weight of your body go down into the ground." I find that a few gentle reminders will induce a slight shift in my body and I will begin to experience a more quiet and settled sensation in my body. I use this state as a kind of platform from which to ask questions or just take a nap or I may scan my body and invite a somatic report on its experience of a situation.

Now imagine:

A bed.
A place for a nap.
A place to sleep.
A place to drift in and out of sleep.
A place to daydream where you can maintain awareness of both
   the conscious and unconscious world.

A place that welcomes and supports stillness.

A place that looks quiet.

A place that suggests we move slowly.

A place where our creative faculty is nurtured and refreshed.

An outdoor place for inactivity.

A place where worn-out people can relax.

A room where the mind naturally slows down.

A place where we are invited to feel heavy.

A room that reminds us of the existence of our bodies.

A garden that reminds us of the needs of our bodies.

At the close of this exercise take a moment to review the images you have received. If any of them move you, make sure you follow your inspiration and record these impressions in some way. The greater the energy these images hold, the more you might want to creatively reflect on and integrate their content.

Body-Centered Design

We have collectively been treating the earth, air, rivers, and oceans the same way we treat our own bodies: as something inferior. Patriarchy has had a long history of believing in masculine superiority over the feminine. There is no logical basis to this, just as there is no logical basis for harming the natural environment. No one thrives in a situation in which they are consistently treated as inferior. We don't like it and the environment surely doesn't. But without looking at these issues psychologically, it is difficult to understand a role for our feelings in design decisions.

The first step toward body-centered design is to simply become aware of your whole body, experiencing the felt sense of the body. Rather than beginning with a focused desire to create or solve, begin with an attitude of readiness to receive an impression from your body. For some, this first step is the most difficult because, as a designer, you are asked not to design or anticipate the design; you are asked to do nothing. Don't take a position toward the problem. Instead, go into your own felt experience of your body and make contact with it in the moment. We usually rush past this experience–I am suggesting that we linger with the feeling. For me, the experience of embodiment is felt. It is a feeling; it's not a think-ing operation, but comes through the channel of feeling.

There are two ways to approach this, one general and the other more specific. Depending on your experience, you may want to experiment with them. In the more general approach, you may inwardly say phrases to yourself such as, "Let go. Set free. Judge not." Inhaling and exhaling normally, try repeating this phrase without any sense of competition or forcing. In the more specific approach, you might begin by asking your jaw to relax. To do this, you need to slow down or relax enough to withdraw your mental attention from your usual habitual responses and bring this atten-tion softly to your body. You need to become interested in your physical self. You need to make contact with the power of your body, the instinctual power of your body to say yes or no.

A series of questions can move you into this place. Am I comfortable? How is my body feeling? Do I feel open? Do I feel tired? Do I believe I have enough energy for the question before me? Am I tired, relaxed, or energized? Once you inwardly feel or hear a yes or no response, you can widen the exploring. Where in the body do I feel constriction? Where do I feel strength, weakness, or expansion? What is my body saying energetically? By asking these simple questions you are shifted to a more body-centered way of knowing. You are bringing the body into the knowing. There is no need to judge any response or get rid of any sensation. The quality of the listening you are capable of giving to any answer determines the fruit of the exercise. Your job is simply to be with whatever sensation is present and to be in caring relationship with it. At that moment you are centered in an awareness of your body and open to its intelligence.

It is to that sensing intelligence that you begin to pose a ques-tion or have a dialogue about your creative work. Whether you are invoking images through drawing, collage, or modeling, your body's voice is brought to the drawing process. There is a different flavor to this experience than that of our normal busy mind, which helps to explain why a different kind of creative result can come from this approach. You become acquainted with a felt sense of the world, the spirit in matter rather then in disembodied spirit. What does it feel like to comfortably breathe and take the world at the same time?

If you "tune into your body," you eventually develop a clear sense of response. You are consciously trying to involve your body in the decision-making process. Like the dowser's rod, your body is able to respond to phenomena that other faculties may not perceive. The body is like a living oracle that, when listened to, naturally gives us access to a whole universe of new sensitivity and creative intelligence. Our bodies is constantly saying yes or no, and, with some patience and sincere interest, this knowing can enrich the design process. The moment the body does not give a clear signal may be the right time to take a real break for the body's sake and return later to the question. When learning a new skill, patience and receptiveness may often be what you need to learn. We don't want to solve problems at the expense of our bodies. We want a kind attitude to the body to be present in the built world.

Letting the body receive the impression and watching the expressive pulsation that follows are important moments in a body-centered approach. This means that during the design stage, when decisions are being made in conjunction with our other resources, the body's ability to broadcast its preferences remains in play. The role of the mind during this approach is twofold. First, the mind remains vigilant: there is no need to react; simply observe what is happening and pay attention to any response. Second, try to be true in recording it. Reflection, analysis, elaboration, and amplification can come later, as required. For some people, this may be the primary way of knowing. A direct kinesthetic and sensing knowledge can form new connections between otherwise unacknowledged phenomena. Given the Western tradition of academic work, this form of knowing has been difficult to test and prove, but we must not dismiss it for that reason. Many of our decisions are made in this way every day. How do we know when we are hungry or thirsty? There is already a high level of trust for this way of knowing–we only need to more consciously access it or tune into it.

Try to remember that your body is a partner in the creative process. Any pianist or dancer will devote considerable attention to posture. Your body needs to allow design decisions to move through it. When I was starting out I worked for a crusty old architect who would tell us that we were holding our pencils too tightly when our work lacked resourcefulness. It is true that a fist can not hold or receive anything. Relax into problem solving by allowing an awareness of your physical posture, your balance, and your center of gravity into your work.

> *A Checklist to Bring to Body-Centered Design*
> Let heaviness be there and let lightness be present.
> Let any feeling of constriction, knots, or tensions be rendered into form.
> Gently become aware of your breathing.
> Is there a difference between the tension on the surface of your body and the tension inside your body? Can you draw an image of this?
> When you draw a space or an artifact, draw its user in a way that includes his or her energetic body—not just a generic body—and gives the body a more living reality.
> Imagine an indoor place that would encourage body-centered awareness.
> Imagine an outdoor place that would encourage body-centered awareness.

As you work, check in with your body. Does the work you are doing agree with your body? Does it make you feel good? Some people report being energized or excited by an image. We all have had such experiences of wellbeing. Where are you now in relation to that feeling? How does your body feel right now?

The Furniture of George Nakashima

Browsing through a favorite bookstore one evening, I came across a stack of remaindered books on sale. From deep in the pile I pulled out a dark cover, *The Furniture of George Nakashima*. I flipped through a few pages and felt a surge of energy go through me. The price was $1.99; I bought it. When I got home I knew I had been searching for this book for a long time. Years later, while living in Philadelphia, I looked up the number of George Nakashima, and the woman who answered the phone told me the studio was closed because he had recently passed away. I put the phone down and waited.

It Takes Time

A year later I called again and learned that the studio had reopened. I can remember my first thought when I rubbed my hand across the furniture: George Nakashima had a different attitude to work than most people. He loved what he did. It was obvious that every piece in the studio was a work of love, every piece was mindfully created before it was made. I felt myself slow down in the presence of this lesson. Patience and reflection were woven so deeply into the objects that creation showed no sign of time. I became more reflective. Time was not the factor driving these creations. Whoever had the time to make these works had recognized and made a great connection with the timeless. Looking at a table, I felt his discipline and the seldom-tasted freedom that comes from such patience. What happens to the purpose of production when time is withdrawn as the great shaper of things? If not time, then who and what will determine the start and end of things? What could replace the clock? I felt my own sense of time expand and dissolve as I looked at the work. These pieces weren't so much about willing an outcome as they were a tacit consent to serve and honor the spiritual part of us that creates. This furniture was a built meditation on the absolute sum of the inner and the outer world. Issues of function seemed unimportant. The energy and poise of each piece felt like an offering and my own sense of the sacred was illuminated in their presence.

Perhaps some things were meant to be built in response to unseen forces, out of time, out of the eye of society and into the lost world of physical things. Why can't the built world call us like a shaman's drum? This isn't the way we do things now. The Jungian analyst James Hollis says the test for soul is found in three things: luminosity, depth, and resonance. I want to add another quality that I found in this studio: the voices of ancestors. The voices of the ones who have come before were strong.

It Takes Space

There seemed to be a great invitation in the work. How do things express their invitations? First the voice of things needs space. Space to resonate. How do you build something that is defined by space? First you bring your own practice of inner space to the process. The invitation of Nakashima's work comes straight from a total acceptance of the material that is being shaped. In this case, I mean this literally because the work is full of voids, gaps, cracks, fissures, and holes. It takes you by surprise that these absences are going to be the voice in the work. But they are and they are very matter-of-fact about it. Somehow they look you in the eye and offer an invitation. Invited to pray by a table full of holes, I began to wonder where creativity comes from and what any of us rests on and what the purpose is of built things. It's as though the emptiness that was embedded in this work was emptying and settling me, and I felt restored. My whole nervous system was reorganized by the subtle invitation to allow all this emptiness to exist.

At the same time, though space fills these works, this doesn't give the work light. Just when you expect lightness, you become aware of the furniture's appetite for darkness. The cracks are like a physical humility. The fissures, wild edges, and dark grains pull at your closed hands. There is a gravity, or what passes for gravity, in this physical world of poetry. You go from feeling like a body in a space to being a body full of space. The furniture is host to caves, doors, tunnels, and deep, dark wells. Expectations are broken. The finished work is full of its original nature. Its making celebrates untamed places. I think somehow our own nature–our own natural, instinctual self–is inevitably tuned to resonate with any other nature that it meets, whether deep in a forest or sitting at a table. There is a brokenness that feels like some kind of acceptance. Something encouraging happens in our psyche through these encounters. All the holes, all the emptiness, all the openings in the work are strangely familiar and this intimacy confers upon our own inner gravity a sense of acceptance. It resonates with something I feel inside myself, something not perfect, finished yet not complete, slowly developed, fragile, not everlasting. Inside us, the gravity of the physical world feels like a sorrow and hope. Perhaps this calibrated chaos holds things together and reminds us of all the mysteries that surround us. The built world can pivot on the presence of the unknown. This work lives through the attention it received in its making, and breathes the reverence it contains.

It Is Dark

Begin with the root, the part of the tree that is left behind when we have taken what we want. The unwanted part of tree is the quiet, restless, physical center of the work. The work pays homage to the unseen forces in things, which are symbolized in the root. This reverence turns a table into an offering, a mystical wheel. What is offered is a tribute to the deep causes of things. As the Zen monk Thich Nhat Hanh has said, "This is like this because that is like that." Our dark and tangled memories are the source of many things. Remembered or not, our roots remain with us and have something to say about the way we will grow. Nakashima leaves the darkness in the table where it can be seen, perhaps discussed, sometimes where it must be eaten. We have to go down inside ourselves to meet this work. Consciously or unconsciously we travel down and into it. It is not found in the broad canopy of leaves that laugh in the wind and offer sweet shade.

When things grow, we concern ourselves with their visible evidence. What happens when we grow in other ways, when we grow through disappointment, sorrow, loss, or regret? Does this count? This built work points to what is not visible, not easily reached, not straightforward, to what lies below in the firm, wet, and difficult darkness. We are in the world of roots, at the bottom of our story. This table is striking in its willingness to bear witness to what lies below. The darkness isn't eliminated, it's included. It brings an altogether different kind of beauty, a beauty that includes the kind of energy that darkens, that shatters. It is the power of this beauty that causes individuals to experience both breakdowns and breakthroughs. Its energy undoes traditions and opinions under the burning light that comes not from above but from within. The root is a dark, flickering tongue and even when you remove it from the ground, it stays surrounded by the luminous, dense gown of the earth. It speaks of secret ways of working with our darkest material.

It Is Full of Opposites

But even this description fails to give a sense of the struggle that has gone into the work. This furniture has been fed by the energy of opposites: the organic and the formal, the light and the dark, the predictable and the chaotic, the raw and the refined, the ordinary and the complex. These opposing forces don't stop until they have run out of breath. At first we have no choice but to resist; sooner or later, after long suffering, we come to appreciate conflicting appetites that are preprogrammed to consume us. We resist, but this is simply our troublemaking way of learning. The only way through the opposites is to accept that conflict exists inside us and to leave it is to leave ourselves. As the American poet Charles Olsen said, we have to become lovers of the difficult. There is always a resolution waiting for us if we can bear the chaos. We may not like it, but enduring it without blame best helps us. But who has the time or inclination to see this struggle in the polished world? Physical poetry, the built world that includes the fact of suffering, shows what these opposites have to teach us. Transcendence comes into material after the designer has endured the tension of the opposites through design.

The art of design is a blend of resolve and sacrifice, of seeing and blindness. We always start with ambition and finish with humility. Through physical poetry we experience the very real possibility that we can be whole in spite of our imperfections and unresolved impulses and expectations. Something has allowed this wooden table to transform into a mirror that forecasts the outcome of inner doubt. The doubts will go on; we are finally ready to be incomplete.

The real tension of opposites creates equanimity. We are waiting for the end of the chaos and instead we discover the necessity of authenticity. The natural world and the built world can create beautiful, hard-won agreements. The grace of these agreements feels like a kind of built poetry.

It Meditates

Living in Philadelphia I found myself returning to the Nakashima studio on Saturdays, attracted to being with these creations. I'd sit in the chairs and stand in the room for hours at a time. I could not leave. Looking back, I would say what attracted me most was the meditation that these works embodied. Not the meditation of being swept out of the body, out of matter, but a meditation in matter. Nakashima's furniture became a meditation on building a life centered in the inseparability of physical experience. Viewed this way everything fell into place and I began to see the possibility that creating could come from this place inside me. This was where wisdom comes from. Why do so few objects or places in the world carry the message of meditation, patience, and reflection? Why does so little of the built world embody the value of contemplation?

Dream

Dreams may contain ineluctable truths, philosophical pronouncements, illusions, wild fantasies, memories, plans, anticipations, irrational experiences, even telepathic visions, and heaven knows what besides.
–C.G. JUNG

Architecture at Night: The Dream

Dreaming is ancient. A recollected dream can deeply affect our sense of self and time, giving the present an unforeseen depth, relating us both to distant ancestors and to new possibilities. A recollected dream can bring us a sense of wonder or dread and reminds us that we belong to something beyond our normal experience of the world. This is because in our normal experience of the world, we are identified with our ego.

The ego is so devoted to its role as decision maker that some liken it to a ruler in a citadel. The ego is not naturally accepting of other points of view, particularly those coming from sources that cannot be controlled. In fact, it can be highly resistant to them. Suggestions and messages from other sources can trigger such strong tactics as defending or counter-attacking; these responses, in turn, are often the triggers of conflict. Yet the covert vocation of the unconscious is to oversee the regular capitulation of the ego's strongly held positions in order to teach the ego to accept sources from outside its limited, self-interested position. This is what we call learning. Such points of view come to us at times from partners, children, and colleagues, but we also have another source: our own dreams. Dreams are completely indifferent to the wishes of the ego, which is why they are so valuable and yet seem so foreign. As designers of the environment we need to take heed of the power of places and things to speak symbolically to the psyche. One way to learn about the relationship between psyche and design is through working with our dreams.

As Jung pointed out, the unconscious is compensatory. It presents a snapshot from the point of view of the unconscious and, therefore, completely bypasses the ego. This why the dream can be at once so powerful and so confusing. It is powerful because of the candor and economy of the unconscious and it is perplexing because although we feel the dream belongs to us in an intimate way, it is not a creation of the ego. In fact, the dream belongs to our own unconscious. The dream always tells us where our life energy wants to go. Its unscripted content is the key to its value and its recollection by our ego is an act of psychic wholeness that represents a victory for the psyche even before the dream is understood.

So deep into our soul do the roots of dreaming go that our ability to understand their relationship to the present, even after years of careful study, may remain charged with difficulty. An image or fragment of a dream may carry a psychic energy that leaves us pondering its meaning for years, or even a for lifetime. The dream expands who we are and allows us to explore the world from a completely different point of view.

The history of dreaming tells us of dreams that have resulted in important creations for scientists and poets alike. According to Dr. Frederick Banting, his discovery of insulin was first presented to him in a dream. In 544 BC, Queen Maya, the Buddha's mother, is reported to have had a dream prophesying the birth of her son. In 1913, Niels Bohr, the Danish physicist, conceived the model of an atom as a nucleus with electrons revolving about it from a dream. The paintings of Salvador Dali, Henri Rousseau, and Jasper Johns are often cited as examples of work whose creative origins were found in dreams. These stories convey only a small fraction of the importance of dreams in our lives, but the role of dreams in creativity has important implications for the built world. Perhaps every great city should have a place dedicated to the miracle of dreaming.

What is clear is that after centuries in which the dream was thought to be an outdated occult fragment of the psyche consigned to uncivilized or unstable peoples, it has re-emerged as a legitimate and modern part of every human being. We are most fortunate not to have lost our capacity to dream because working with our dreams may prove to be uniquely helpful in allowing us to live more sane lives in the modern world. Freud stated that the dream was the royal road to the unconscious. Strangely, it also has the possibility of being a direct and valuable road to the renewal of the built world. Dreams are rich with architectural artifacts and settings whose meanings can help cool our reactions to the problems we live with, and give us hope in the face of those we think we cannot bear.

The Structure of the Dream

> The whole dream-work is essentially subjective, and a dream is a theatre in which the dreamer is himself the scene, the player, the prompter, the producer, the author, the public and the critic.
> –C.G. JUNG

The interpretation of a dream is a spiritual craft. We need to shift our usual way of looking so that we are more involved in learning to connect with the mystery and many moods of the dream.

Dreams, no matter how simple or surreal, have a beginning, middle, and end, just like any other narrative. A dream usually begins with a very particular description of a place. The purpose of the "setting" in the dream is literally to "set the scene" for the action that follows. In dreams, we find the setting being used symbolically to express the dreamer's psychological place in the world. It tells us where the dreamer is, but from the point of view of the unconscious. For example, I may be sitting in my old kitchen, which may point toward the need for me to assimilate something from the past, or I may be walking across a busy street, which may point to the need for me to change my perspective. The opening of the dream narrative locates the psychological orientation of the dream, and when we look at the setting of the dream, we find ourselves examining places that are either built or natural. The setting may be familiar or exotic, real or richly imagined, but it will always point to where we are in our unconscious.

The way a real setting is used symbolically by the psyche to present information about the places in our lives where we are unconscious began to interest me. I wondered about the role of the setting because it is so important to the meaning of the dream and it is so important to work done by architects and designers. From basements to grand boulevards, from modern airports to mountains, there is no limit to the kind of settings found in dreams. And these are the very settings designers struggle with when they try to bring meaningful places to life through their work.

I began to think that even though our society essentially dismisses the meaning of architecture and the value of place-making, it is obvious that the psyche is tuned in to its importance. And it therefore follows that the modern designer has a key role to play in not only designing the built world, but in also creating settings for the dreaming that comes from our inner world. Everything we make exists in the built world and the dream world. Our conscious mind may be busy taking a photograph at the cottage or drinking coffee in the kitchen or angrily driving to work, but our unconscious mind is aware of absorbing the experience from a symbolic angle. The cities and landscapes we inhabit are experienced consciously and unconsciously, exactly the same way we create them. Just as centuries of place-making are available to our dreaming mind, so too new creations offer settings that speak to states of mind yet to be dreamed.

Working with the Dream

One night, when I was traveling by car through rural Arizona, I had a dream about tree roots. In this dream I found my house full of these extraordinary pieces of wood. When I woke up I felt happy—there was something rich, dark, and abundant about these pieces of wood. Later that day I was surprised to see in the local newspaper an advertisement for furniture made from the roots of trees. I became excited and knew I had to go there. The place was hard to find, well off the main street in an unmarked shed, but as soon as I entered the workshop I felt deeply moved and at one with everyone and everything there.

The branches, burls, roots, and massive planks were an earthly and surreal feast. I had been ill for several years and this workshop was like medicine. The roots and burls were from manzanilla trees, juniper, and other high-desert species. They looked unworldly, almost fragile, yet they were also full of the earth and very robust in unexpected ways. They looked like congealed gasses. Great burls that had formed beneath the earth in the gut of the tree symbolized everything I was feeling but could not express. They contained the beautiful difficult beginning of things. I bought several pieces of wood that seemed to express mysterious states of transformation. Since that day I have always searched for tree roots when I travel. I collect the roots of trees; I can't stop searching for them. My fascination with and connection to tree roots is similar to the centuries-old veneration of stones in Chinese and Japanese land-scape. The tradition of the Chinese scholar's rock also testifies to the creative energy that can be found in every kind of object.

When we think of the roots of a tree from the point of view of producing a consumable resource, it has no purpose. When forests are harvested, anything below the stump often remains untouched. The roots are not suitable for commercial lumber. But from the point of view of the tree, the root is essential—it holds the tree in place in the earth, delivers nutrients, prevents erosion, and offers habitats to many creatures. We know that root structures are equal to or larger then the visible part of the tree. In this way, the roots can symbolize the unconscious—unseen, yet entirely essential for the healthy life of the organism.

There are three elements in dreams that need to be listened to and investigated: the narrative, the symbol, and the context. What seems banal in the built world can become a very provocative symbol in a dream. The unconscious releases its meaning like the perfume of an exotic flower; the dining-room table where we used to sit, the light in the basement that we can see through a grate in the floor–all of these everyday objects carry meaning.

A client recounted her dream about running down the greatest boulevard in the city, which links the center of government to the water. The first thing she said was that she didn't even like that street, rarely went on it-even avoided it. She didn't like the govern-ment in power and found the street "dead." In fact, she thought that the dream wasn't about her at all, that she only dreamed about herself on that particular street because she had been there only a few weeks before. The dream meant nothing to her, she said. But why had the psyche selected that specific street and the image of the legislative building? I asked. The dreamer had been all over the city in the last few weeks and had walked down dozens of streets, so why had the psyche selected the street that runs from the house of power to the open sea? And why during the day and not the night? She may not have liked the street or the government, but her unconscious was trying to communicate that the city, through its architecture, had an important symbolic message for her about the issue of power. If she was willing to spend more time with her dream, she might have discovered that the city was telling her where she was psychologically. The city was directing her to take more responsibility for her own power. For all of who live in it, the city is home to more than our busy lives; it is home to our unconscious. Bringing dreams to conscious reflection not only enhances our relationship to the unconscious, but also opens us to designing the symbolic world, the world of meaning where energy and phenomena touch.

EXERCISE

If you are not able to remember dreams, take a moment to ask yourself if you really want to remember them. It is important to look at your motives when doing this. If you have a sincere interest in remembering your dreams, then go to a store and choose a notebook to record your dreams. Before going to sleep, make sure the book and a pen, and perhaps a flashlight, are conveniently located next your bed. When you get into bed, remind yourself that you have decided to pay attention to your dreams. All of these actions signal to your unconscious your will-ingness to receive its messages. These are the first steps to making a bridge to the unconscious.

If you already remember your dreams or have dream images, begin to keep a journal of your dreams. If you experience an image that has a numinous quality—an artifact or image that draws your interest—then just go ahead and draw the image. Go with what moves you. If any object or narrative seems overwhelming, then seek the help of someone experi-enced in working with these elements. It is wise to not underestimate the importance of these experiences, so when you are unsure, I would suggest working with a competent guide.

Symbols

A sign is always less than the thing it points to, and a symbol is always more than we can understand at first sight. Therefore we never stop at the sign but go on to the goal it indicates; but we go on with the symbol because it promises more than it reveals.
–C.G. JUNG

When I got home from a two-week meditation retreat, I was invited to a dinner party in the most distant suburb of north London. I realized that it would take more then an hour to get there by bus and train, and set out without much enthusiasm. On the train, I fell into a light sleep and arrived at the last station and walked another 15 minutes before arriving at the street I was looking for, a 19th-century street of two-storey houses that spread unremarkably through the suburbs of London. A few minutes later I stood in front of my host's house. I walked up a few steps and reached the door, which was not locked, and entered a vestibule. It was a very tall narrow space, completely wallpapered with beautifully drawn red roses that seemed to suddenly intensify before blossoming inside me. My heart become warm and I began to cry. Something that had started at the meditation retreat two weeks earlier was completed in this little space. Ever since that experience in the vestibule of roses, a part of me has lived open to the symbolic quality of the built world. Looking back, I feel that something inside me was initi-ated into the symbolic world in that small space.

We forget that the built world is also a symbolic world. The door, the staircase, the act of opening and closing, the way a column is upright, a pool of still water reflecting what is above–all of these ordinary "built" conditions are also symbols potentially filled with the latent energy of psychic transformation. The very substance of architectural imagination is deeply related to our ability to imagine the world symbolically. This symbolic potential suggests that there is always a second project, a double, "a ghost, a spirit and shadow world" embedded within all material, natural or built. It waits there until it is called upon to speak to us through the dream.

Dreams confirm that the world of efficiency and convenience is not enough for our modern psyche; we need a world of meaning. We have an appetite for meaning. When a sign on the highway tells us "100 miles to Dallas," our intellect may be satisfied because we can compute the time required to complete our journey, but there are other parts of us that are ignored by this message. If we are returning home and anticipating conflict, the sign will have a very different meaning than it will if we are visiting a new grandchild.

At night we dream of places and settings that illuminate what we need to consciously integrate and incorporate in order to move toward our own wholeness. But because dreams present their point of view from the unconscious, we often can't make head or tail of them. To understand the dream we need to enter the symbolic world. We cannot interpret a dream or a symbol with our ego. Symbols from the dream may stimulate years of research and scholarship, and the meaning of the dream is rarely a simple matter. The dream, with its narrative and symbols, belongs to a particular context, the life of the dreamer.

There was a time when the appearance of things was more predictable. We all recognize a 19th-century museum or city hall or courthouse. There is no need for a large sign labeling the institution. A century later and these same institutions are unpredictable in their appearance. We can no longer agree upon what a courthouse or school should look like. Yet when the built world falls back on images that have exhausted their meaning, the entire society experiences a loss. Today we have no choice but to ask questions that go deeper into the designer in order to find out the identity of things. And this makes perfect sense because we are asking deeper questions about ourselves. What exactly does a school do? What is our relationship to learning or, in the case of a courthouse, what is justice? We need to take these issues and clarify our personal relationship to the institution. While this may seem like an annoyance to some, without this level of commitment it is easy to assign the task to a criteria of function. If we are willing to bring our personal felt experience into the process of design the built world will become a meaningful container for the psychological quest that is alive in so many people. As individuals change through recognizing and learning from their unconscious, so too must the built world go through a transformation that acknowledges what is meaningful to the individual.

While designers are involved in understanding how to support their structures, these same structures are involved in supporting different aspects of the occupant. One of these is the part of us that needs to live in a world with meaning. And this aspect of meaning is communicated through symbols.

The Symbolic World of Masculine and Feminine

Men and women, and masculine and feminine qualities, regularly appear in our dreams. They can be both known and unknown figures, communicated through symbols and through energetic qualities. Seen energetically, Our Father Who Art in Heaven and the energies of Mother Nature are always in play in the world. Great symbols always offer the designer significant lessons and resources.

Masculine: Our Father Who Art in Heaven

The animating and enlivening principle of spirit has long been associated with the masculine principle, as is consciousness and the intellect. The masculine built world is symbolized by artifacts and spaces devoted to action, movement, and work. When they are overused or overvalued, these masculine principles result in patriarchal conditions. The geometric towers and skyscrapers that define our modern cities symbolize the overwhelming influence of masculine principles in the built world; the collapse of these buildings may speak to the end of the overvaluation of these same patriarchal beliefs. The other great masculine artifact of our modern cities is infrastructure. These enormous constructions are seldom thought of as "designed," yet in their self-absorbed rationality they express the masculine, as do many performance-based workspaces such as offices, fast-food restaurants, and laboratories. Environments that show no regard for nurturing life, or that ignore basic human longings are evidence of overloaded masculine traits and are common throughout contemporary suburban and urban developments. Factories and malls that imperiously impose themselves on the agricultural land surrounding most cities represent the one-sided patriarchal values that grip modern planning debates.

While they are usually the product of municipal or regional planning design studies, these environments signify a major victory of infrastructure and organization, characteristics necessary when going into battle, but less significant if the goal is to ennoble a human-centered life. The habitual overvaluation of one quality, usually the masculine, translates into abstract and counterintuitive spaces that have become the norm in North America. The resulting alienation and a lack of "place" are symptoms of the one-sided thinking that continues to dominate most urban design. Tools and their modern equivalents, which we see in the latest technological devices, belong to this category and speak to the penetrating role of the intellect that accompanies many of these inventions.

Feminine: Mother Nature

All those artifacts and places that are hollow, offer refuge, and can be filled through inhabitation or use symbolize the feminine built world. Churches are considered feminine because they contain the spirit of the Father. The unconscious is considered feminine because it is the source of all things or, as Jung liked to say, "the womb of the arts"–it is infinite and from it, consciousness emerges. Artifacts as diverse as ships, walled cities, public spaces, niches, gardens, and homes belong to a category of objects and places that have associations with the feminine. While men may be thought of as "king of the castle," they are usually only in charge of fixing the house, while all the decisions that relate to the inside the house have traditionally been the domain of the feminine. Places that offer refuge and protection draw from the symbolic world of feminine traits, as do sensual places like spas, where our bodies feel an immediate and natural kinship. The feminine experience is alive in the built world when we feel a sense of belonging or "at oneness" with our surroundings. A reverence for materials and the carefully considered relationship between different materials is often central to communicating this sensibility. It can be seen in the crafted moments of design in which a well-detailed seam or joint is revealed or the decision to use color acknowledges the emotional richness we all share. The purpose of these generalizations is not to suggest a simplistic picture of what is masculine or what is feminine or to declare that one set of characteristics is more necessary than another. They are intended to give the designer more awareness of the potential for the symbolic dimension to underpin serious design decisions.

Masculine and Feminine

At a deeper level, these symbols have a dynamic that is explained by Carl Jung's idea that men and women have contra-sexual male and female qualities. This means that men have unconscious feminine traits, which he termed the anima, while women carry unconscious masculine qualities that he called the animus. The words anima and animus don't carry the same meaning, nor are they meant as indication of gender, but point to a cluster of qualities that are psychological in character. We can see this idea on a genetic level where science has discovered that men and women carry genes of the opposite sex within their bodies.

In Eastern cultures, the Tao symbol, with its yin and yang energies, expresses the same idea. The Tao symbol, consisting of a circle divided into two equal portions, each containing an element of the other, indicates that all of creation is composed of two interdependent energies that interact and seek harmony. In regard to psychological functioning, men are predominately yang but contain a yin aspect. Women, while predominately yin, contain an element of yang. This supports the idea that human beings are psychologically androgynous with latent inner masculine and feminine energies awaiting development.

Yang energy is masculine and is described as light, dry, directed, focused, logical, and action-oriented. Yin energy is feminine and described as dark, moist, diffuse, vague, intuitive, and receptive. A simple example of the way these two energies are combined may be found in the act of walking. First we need to learn to stand and get grounded, which is feminine energy. This is followed by the energy used to step forward, which is masculine. In the creative process, we experience both of these energies. A creative cycle of work involves receptivity or containment followed by a pulsation of something new that inspires us and moves us forward, which is in turn contained again before another wave of new images or ideas comes forth.

What interests me is the question of how these unconscious traits find their way into the built world and how designers can learn to work more consciously to bring these covert characteristics into their work. Contra-sexual traits represent ways of experiencing the world that are often excluded from our understanding of a design problem. Yet what makes a design great is the way it manages to touch us precisely because it embraces and transcends and makes conscious what had once been thought of as irreconcilable opposites.

Cities that have lost their feminine qualities are full of places where people no longer want to live. These places have often been spoiled by large-scale infrastructure or ruined by political willfulness that leaves us with no choice but to resort to extra policing for life to feel possible. Public places that graciously draw us out of our separateness offer us the setting we need to gather in peace and watch life unfold. These kinds of places, like Pailey Park in New York, are nearly impossible to quantify to a patriarchal civic bureaucracy, yet they offer a refuge that fundamentally understands our human longing to connect with others and ourselves. Airports, when they are overly concerned with complex issues of organizational movement, ignore the deep-seated anxiety that accompanies the modern experience of travel. When offices become too concerned with performance, mysteriously, performance declines. How did the culture of design evolve to the point that our schools often resemble factories or prisons?

When the symbolic masculine and feminine elements of design work together, their own properties are expanded. Bridges are symbols of this co-operation because, in one gesture, they elegantly combine extension and connection. Amenity, the idea that an artifact, space, or place can be capable of an act of good will, is a vastly underappreciated resource of design. Arcades, canopies, generous thresholds, porches, and urban-scaled stairways can all be designed to perform a service beyond their original use. The accumulation of these acts of kindness and generosity are like medicine to the urban soul. One look at environments where these thoughtful moments have been lost and we realize that the fragile quality of human experience is easily sacrificed and ignored. A disregard for the rich and subtle emotional spectrum inevitably leads us to the conclusion that emotions and less measurable experiences are not relevant ways of knowing the world. Who would have thought that something as simple as natural light should become a rare experience in the working world? Banal environments rapidly beget the erosion of the felt world.

The choice of a material can sometimes send a signal that no amount of formal invention can express. How does a designer communicate belonging or comfort without using a sign? The airport in Copenhagen has wooden floors. After a long, disembodying transatlantic flight, it was a surprise and then a deeply comforting experience to arrive back on earth and find wooden floors under my feet. I felt immediately grounded and assured of the value of my senses.

Unfortunately the modern landscape repeatedly dismisses our sensitivity to belonging and so it is no wonder that a part of our nature, the ability to feel vulnerable and our need to respond and embrace place, is eroded. These instincts are being dulled by a lack of use. We forget the value of sensitivity until we unconsciously shut down that part of ourselves. Incrementally, we lose personal way-finding skills and reduce our resources for decision making. It is rare to find feminine qualities in the large projects that increasingly make up our urban and suburban landscape. How many monuments have you visited that you would call feminine in character? The entire arc of 20th-century urban planning took a long and painful detour through a patriarchal fascination with efficiency and geometry. We are only now recovering an awareness of the reality of human psychological needs. A concern for fit and detail and a sensibility that includes materiality as a fundamental aspect of the designer's palette communicates with the feminine. Where we don't feel related to our world we find a lack of the feminine. It's only over the last 10 years that we have seen any significant number of female professionals in the architectural or planning professions. The world of engineering and construction is trying to reach this modest level of participation, but this may take many more years. Therefore, if we are to see any meaningful change in the built environment in the foreseeable future, it may be men who have to bring their feminine aspects into the act of design.

The National Museum of Anthropology, Mexico City

The National Museum of Anthropology in Cholpoultepec Park, Mexico City is a remarkable achievement. Designed by the architect Ramirez Vazquez, it was completed in 1964 to house the great collection of artifacts that tell the story of the peoples who lived in the land we now call Mexico. The modern galleries are generous and possess a calm evenness that never feels severe.

But the true heart of the place is not revealed until you enter the enormous courtyard. There stands the great canopy fountain. Nothing prepares you for the scale of this object. It is immediately too large and then just right, then perhaps not large enough! It is a construction that seems entirely mythical. It made me feel big and small. It moved me and I wanted to stand under it. When I got closer I became cooler and more expansive. Its scale is as improbable and irrefutable as history itself. It is speaking to me on so many levels that I need to touch it, or I fear it may collapse. It is proud and strong, sheltering and lovely. Reason built it but could make no argument for it. I like to imagine the architect explaining his case to the client for why the courtyard will not be complete without this act of creative truth. The place feels like a song or poem created by Pablo Neruda. Water pours down the bronzed column created by José and Thomas Chavez Morado that depicts the history of Mexico. The water splashes like children laughing, which somehow makes the heat in the courtyard a distant memory. When such structures are built, the gods celebrate; these paradoxes bring heaven to earth. At first, the structure seems all about the sky and the great gift of shade offered by the broad canopy, but eventually I began to see the place differently. I began to see a great column rising from the earth, from the parched courtyard of the museum. It is a courageous gesture that speaks to the mind, body, and spirit. This courtyard inspires endurance and patience. The high canopy gathers cool breezes. To stand beneath this artifact is to travel between worlds. The ancestors gather here. The center of the world is alive and well here. It is a symbol and we can never finish with it.

The Symbolic House

The house is a common symbol in dream analysis. Its many rooms are seen to have particular meanings, as do its setting and architectural style. It is also useful to look closely at the house because it is such a universal symbol. Many institutions are looked upon as houses–houses of worship, or palaces of sport. I offer the following comments as a point of departure for your own enquiries into the meaningful design of the house. At the same time, they may serve as useful reflections when these rooms appear symbolically in your own dreams.

The house can symbolize the state of the whole psyche, while the rooms that appear in a dream are parts of yourself that make up the whole of the psyche. You may live in a basement apartment and dream of living in the White House as easily as the US president may dream of living in a basement apartment. The living room is where we do our living and relating and refers to new potentials in everyday life, while a scene involving a dining room or restaurant may point to what we are trying to assimilate. The kitchen is where we prepare and create the food we eat to nourish ourselves, and so may symbolize where we put ideas together. The bedroom is where we go to sleep and become unconscious; it may also refer to where we become one with whatever our partner symbolizes. The computer room refers to the thinking function. Seeing through a window points to seeing through a situation. People seeing into your room or house may point to a need for boundaries or privacy. Closets represent the part of the unconscious where we keep things hidden away when we are not using them. The bathroom symbolizes a place where we express our feelings, and where we relieve ourselves (urination) of unconscious content (defecation) that we don't need anymore. The bath and shower symbolize a new spiritual attitude and are related to the bathroom's role in rituals of cleanliness and purification. Staircases allow us to travel to different levels. When we go to another level in a dream, we are connecting to another part of ourselves. For example, when descending we are working out past programming. Going upstairs is symbolic of coming to a new understanding. Where does the staircase lead? The new understanding will relate to where the staircase leads you. A spiral staircase represents a point of view understood from a new level. The attic represents intuition, as does the roof. Being at the top of the house we get the big picture, which allows us to see all the possibilities. The basement symbolizes the unconscious. It often has a furnace, which provides heat for the house. Heat symbolizes warmth in your life and may open the door to recognizing physical symptoms or concerns about physical energy.

In the dream, a front yard indicates that you are conscious of the situation the dream is referring to. The garden can be a place of unity. The walls around it may indicate privacy and protection of the self. If you have found new rooms, this points to new possibilities within you. The front door points to conscious understanding, while the back door may point to something in the unconscious that needs to be examined. Locked doors indicate understandings that are still not conscious. Hallways symbolize transitions. Hotels symbolize temporary situations, while apartments point to a compartmentalized part of the self. The house in your dream will symbolize the way you are living your life. In a dream, going home indicates that you are reconnecting with yourself.

These comments give the briefest glimpse of and introduction to the world of dreams and their symbols. I want to give some flavor of the possibility for designers to engage more than material when they undertake a project. In the design of everything lies the symbolic value of the artifact as well as its material quality. The design of a bathroom is more than tiles and plumbing. Symbolically, we are dealing with rituals and conditions of renewal and purification. In order to connect with a more soulful level of design, we need to be aware of the power of places and things to move us, and this is most directly appreciated through experiencing the symbolic world.

Belongings, Possessions

There is always something we would like to add to what we already own and things we need to get rid of. We are engaged in a busy exchange of keeping, acquiring, storing, displaying, and discarding.

The word "belongings" says it best. There are things that we develop strong attachments to and there are things we are no longer tied to. We have a sense that things not only belong to us, they have acquired a capacity to connect us to a place. They are part of why we feel we belong. Objects help us to belong because they carry an aspect of our emotional lives; they lift the space out of the realm of utility and help us to cross over some subtle threshold that divides utility from warmth. The architect Le Corbusier's famous statement that a house is a machine for living in, while perhaps directed at technology and issues of production, became a powerful voice in the making of the modern idea of home.

We personalize objects, or as these objects age under our care, they acquire special properties. A room filled with our belongings is enhanced. We demand less in hotel rooms than we would in our own world because it is temporary. When we travel we bring what we need for the trip in a practical sense, but there are always things we bring that have nothing to do with being practical.

A friend told me she didn't like her home, but she didn't know why. She asked me to visit her there and see if anything could be done to make the place more comfortable. She had lived in the apartment for several years and it had everything she needed to be physically comfortable: a big sofa facing a big TV, lots of pictures on the wall. We talked for a while, but the problem didn't seem to be the arrangement of her furniture. When I asked her about her favorite things, she began to talk with great reverence and enthusiasm about a collection of antique beaded handbags she had received from her grandfather. When I asked to see them, she left the room to get them from a big chest of drawers where they were stored. She returned with four very delicate and colorful bags and immediately began to tell me stories about her grandfather and everything he had meant to her. When she finished I asked if she would like to arrange them on the wall of her living room, like a kind of painting or wall hanging. The idea surprised her, but she was willing to try it. Their presence on the wall changed everything. The ancestors were present and so was her love of her grandfather. Her feelings mattered. The little collection of bags did not constitute a renovation or significant addition, but they initiated a significant shift in her home. She now felt she had permission to express herself in her own home.

EXERCISE

It is valuable to do an inventory not of what you own, but of what matters to you. Where is it in the house and why is it there? What is the history of the object? Where does it come from? What does it mean?

EXERCISE: THINKING ABOUT SETTING AS SYMBOL

One way to begin to learn from the settings in our dreams is to draw those places we remember from our dreams. Doing this involves us in pondering the felt sense of those places and perhaps asking questions of those settings–an exotic house or a ragged hut–as if they were friendly strangers. "What has brought you to this dream? What have you to tell me?" Ask yourself what associations you have with the image. Remember to give yourself time to listen and reflect and write down each response. The old saying "Haste is the Devil" is very true.

EXERCISE: THINKING ABOUT PLACE AS SYMBOL

Sit or imagine yourself in a favorite place. Is there a way to have a relationship with the place as symbol? A relationship with the symbol? On a symbolic level, why does this place attract you? What part of you feels sheltered or supported? A simple way to begin this is to bring a dictionary of symbols with you and take a walk to a place you like to go. When you get to your destination, go back over your walk, looking up the symbolic meaning of the artifacts or kinds of places you were attracted to.

EXERCISE: EXAMINING ARTIFACT AS SYMBOL

Think about what is your most prized possession. It may be a bicycle, a carving, or a chair. How did you acquire it? What does it allow you to do? What does it ask of you? If you have difficulty choosing something, think back to your childhood and see if there was a favorite activity or plaything.

EXERCISE: LEARNING TO RELATE TO SYMBOLS

Draw a door that opens onto your life at this moment.
Draw a door that opens onto your past.
Draw a window that allows you to see into the future.
What size would it be? What color? What material? Is it heavy or light? Is there an inscription above the door?

Designers' Dream Work

Artistic creations perform for society what the dream performs for the individual.
–E. EDINGER

An architectural student in her final year, Sally was stuck. She was undecided about what her thesis project should be. A daughter of a Holocaust survivor, she had discussed designing a memorial, but that challenge didn't feel quite right. For some time she had been unsure where to find inspiration. She mentioned that she had repeatedly had the same dream for years, and so I suggested that she might try drawing images from a dream. The next time we met, Sally showed me a series of drawings that immediately had everyone's attention. These drawings were images from dreams she remembered having as child. I never heard the complete dream narrative, but many of the images had to do with hiding and, indeed, her family's survival during the war had rested in part on their ability to evade capture by hiding. A very gifted artist, Sally had shown these drawings to her uncle, who had until then been unwilling to discuss his experience. Somehow these images allowed a new attitude to emerge. He began to open up to her and more drawings followed. From her uncle's description, Sally drew his hiding place during the war. It was a space created in the expanded thickness of a wall. This sparked new conversations with her mother, who described other hiding places that Sally then drew.

After some time to reflect, Sally decided to design an adoption center. Somehow this project fit her journey and allowed her to not have to live the untold stories of her mother or uncle. The spark for her final project came from her dream. The creative momentum and power of the project was palpable. She made a conscious attempt to extend the dream-like images into the new project. Not only did she feel grounded and inspired while working on the project, but people who saw the completed work recognized at once that there was a soulful and inspired basis for the work. Everyone was moved by her transcription, and the result was a beautiful project. What I learned from the experience was the possibility for a design project to have integrity and an integrating influence on its designer. The act of design can reach backward to move forward into new places of meaning and reconciliation.

The direct way to reflect on the importance of the symbolic power of architectural language is to look at your own dreams. There are therapists who are trained to help you to work creatively and safely with your dreams. Dreams deliver precious psychological insight as well as direct creative inspirations. They often give fully ripened clues about creative direction. Centuries of recorded dreams contain numerous examples of people like you and me having their lives deeply affected by the images of their dreams. This is not to claim that every dream contains images of a building waiting to be designed, but the dream will help us to know if the creative process we are following is helping or harming us.

Any image from a dream is a symbol and in that sense can be worked with, played with, and psychically unfolded. Often, the most helpful response to an image is to work directly with it. Draw it, paint it, model it; perhaps write a letter to it. If a particular symbol appears in your dreams–for example a vase or a doorway– make a model or a copy of it. Perhaps the symbol is an object you have in a drawer and you can carry it with you for a few days. Let the symbol speak to you, get a feel for its sense of gravity. Listen to what the image has to say. What we are doing at these moments is relating to an aspect of our own nature. We are learning to live as though the unconscious aspect of life is real. The law here seems to be that if good energy goes into the relationship with the unconscious, it will be more inclined to offer back its own images and sense of direction.

The dream can reveal a rarely experienced form of an event: its depth. And this teaches us that what seems like the covert or hidden view of something is actually the holistic point of view, the view that includes the unconscious side of life. The unconscious is not about ignorance, but about the unseen, the missing point of view, the needed "otherness" that reveals the whole. The dream faithfully reports this; it has been programmed to do this. Its uncanny sense of truth probably evolved from our intense moments of admitting complete helplessness. When our own known resources are unable to solve a problem, our sense of helplessness forms into a single appeal for help and activates something deep in the psyche itself. If the function of the dream was not to inform us of anything new, we would likely have stopped dreaming.

Even if you don't want to relate to the products of the unconscious, even if you believe this approach does not apply to your way of working, you may still find yourself dreaming about being lost in a part of the city you have never enjoyed or you may find yourself dreaming about a part of the house you rarely visit. In a dream you may witness the collapse of an entire city block or conversely you may visit a part of the city and feel uneasy as it reminds you of a scene from some old dream. The ego cannot be expected to understand and solve everything. There will always be a choice about whether to consciously work with dreams and their images, but there is no choice about whether it happens. It does happen. You may not remember your dreams, but others may dream of being lost in your house or joyous in one of your creations. Your design work exists in the psychic world whether you are willing to accept this or not.

Frank Ghery in Berlin

The DG Bank headquarters in Berlin obeys the ordinances of the city peacefully enough, although it does give off a faint sense of tension and restraint—a subtle protest seems to rest on its skin. It occupies an entire block and, like other structures of this size, contains a courtyard. It is not until one enters the courtyard that things make sense. If you imagine the inner space of the building as the courtyard, the covert nature of the project emerges. Consciously, the building is following orders, but unconsciously it has something very different to say. Waiting for you in the courtyard are all things we are forbidden to express on the street. It houses a giant sculptural horse head of glass and steel, a great symbol of the basic life force, unconstrained, like some moment between freedom and rage. The public face of the city goes along with the reasonable manners that your relatives might expect. The courtyard tells us that repressed unconscious energy has to go somewhere and often it goes inside. There it can sit until it becomes our mad twin. The dark shadow that rises from the torqued and sculpted metal and glass like the wild head of a horse on fire painted by Kokoshka is the built shadow of Berlin. It is also—effortlessly—the conference center of a bank! It also looks like a goalie mask left too long in a microwave oven. Everyone who enters walks through this beautiful and terrible shriek of history. Surrealism taught us that many unresolved emotions can exist within a single canvas. Disturbing conditions often need to see the light of day if they are to change; there is a value in learning to face things as they are. But first we need to see what lies behind the walls we have made.

Shadow

"I followed you."

"I saw no one."

"That is what you may expect to see when I follow you."

–SHERLOCK HOLMES (SIR ARTHUR CONAN DOYLE)

Psychologically, the shadow is a positive or negative aspect of the self that is unconscious and, therefore, is not under the control of the ego. Given its elusive character and its profound capacity to generate trouble, the shadow requires particularly careful reading. This chapter sketches out the way our psychological shadow affects the built world through its impact on the designer and how designers can learn to bring their own shadow into the act of designing.

The shadow is deceptive; it is a master of disguise. Because it is unacknowledged, it always seems to belong to others. We see it everywhere, but can never find it because it actually belongs to our own unconscious. The way we become aware of our shadow is through a mechanism Jung called projection, an involuntary psychic act whereby we cast our shadow onto others. This act is always charged with energy and it is this energy we have the opportunity to reclaim for our own lives through the therapeutic process of "owning" the shadow. The direct way to discover our own shadow is to notice what we find most annoying in others. Chances are that the traits you find most irritating or overwhelming in others point to your own shadow aspects. Keep in mind that our projections usually involve judgments that have us see ourselves as greater than others (inflation) or worse than others (deflation). Neither position is actually true.

When we see others who appear successful or creative we may be swept away by their opinions and forget our own talents because we may have grown up never hearing that we were creative or could be successful. By owning this example of positive projection we can allow ourselves to connect with our repressed creativity and begin to become more confident about our own abilities. Another example might find us being judgmental whenever someone around us becomes angry because we may have grown up in a home where anger was forbidden and repressed our own anger. Instead of then judging others, we need to get in touch with our own repressed anger so that we can use its energy at appropriate times and in appropriate ways.

Jung stated that we unconsciously project to the extent that we have not consciously assimilated the shadow's presence. Inevitably, therefore, what we like least in ourselves we will unconsciously repress and project onto others. This act of repressing takes considerable energy to maintain, as does the act of sustaining a judgmental projection. Not only is this energy lost to us, it prevents us from having compassion for anyone–including ourselves.

This need to assimilate our shadow aspect is easy to write about, but is difficult to achieve. It is difficult because it means accepting longstanding parts of ourselves that have been labeled unacceptable. The value of the shadow to the designer is that it often presents us with new ways to understand our problems. For example, when we draw a building two-dimensionally, there is no shadow. The building exists only as a façade. Not until we incorporate the shadow does the building become three-dimensional and gain depth. In other words, incorporating the dark shadow can often bring the quality of transformation to our work in the form of new images and ideas.

The shadow is within us, but because we don't search for it there, our only choice is to project it out onto others or into the world and build it. Because the shadow belongs to individuals, it can manifest itself in all things that are created by individuals. It is found in collective entities like business organizations, institutions, and governments. The shadow of society is a massive force, an accumulation of unconscious aspects projected onto others, onto our cities, and onto the way we treat the natural world. It is found in our institutions, in our public spaces, and in our homes. In a sense, everything created contains the unconscious imprint of its makers and carries their shadows. In an individual, this may appear as a sudden stream of judgment; in society, it manifests when those in positions of power collectively refuse to acknowledge vast depressing stretches of city because of the unconscious judgments they project onto those places and the people who live there. The contemporary trend to "heal" toxic sites, be they residential or industrial, represent positive examples of reclaiming the collective civic shadow.

One example of shadow that has been assimilated into the built world over the last 30 years is interesting because it may herald a shift of awareness as profound as any of the great technological inventions of the past. Since the 1970s, for the first time, building legislation requires architects to design for the needs of physically challenged citizens. Public buildings and public spaces must now be accessible to all citizens, regardless of their physical capacities, so that all can enjoy equal access to goods and services. While "barrier-free design"–the provision of ramps and special bathrooms and Braille in elevators, represents a modest undertaking as a percentage of total building cost, the question as to why this need has taken so long to acknowledge is no small issue. What were we thinking when we designed places and buildings whose thresholds prohibited access to the elderly, to children, or to the injured? It is not as though old age, illness, children, or physical disability did not exist before 1970, but society was apparantly unable to collectively acknowledge the suffering of a physical limitation or feel the ache of exclusion.

Unconsciously, we seem to have believed that when the human body did not meet certain standards, it was imperfect and substandard and from the point of view of the built world, simply did not exist. The truth is we that have never been able to incorporate imperfection and suffering in our buildings or environment because most of us cannot accept it in ourselves. It belongs to our personal shadow, so we, until relatively recently, had no choice but to project it into our collective creations. As a society we are strangers to the honest messages that arise from the seemingly less civilized aspects of ourselves. That this is not a modern stance, but an attitude rooted in centuries of design points to the depth of these unconscious beliefs.

Rather than see our bodies and emotions as honest and trustworthy messengers when adequately heard, we have been trained to turn away from their signals. And though fate always brings problems back, we remain inexperienced when it comes to recognizing and incorporating our own projected shadow. Avoidance of the shadow is epidemic in a society like ours, a society addicted to perfection. The parts of us that cause us to suffer are usually treated as inferior, and they consequently receive less attention. The symbols of the inferior aspects of the self are found everywhere in modern cities. The homeless stand begging for food and shelter beside shiny new baseball stadiums. They are like the handicapped of 30 years ago; though they walk among us, we act as if they don't exist because we don't want to acknowledge their suffering. Jung pointed out that the psychology of the masses is rooted in the psychology of the individual. We need to bring a new perspective to the built world, one that is based on observing our creations, be they artifacts, infrastructure, or places from the point of view of the psyche and, in particular, from the point of view of the shadow. I wonder if the inclusion of the physically challenged and the homeless in the built world might be preparing us to acknowledge a more subtle but equally pervasive affliction that fills our lives and, therefore, our cities: mental illness.

Depression, abuse, anxiety, loneliness, and bipolar disorder are not just familiar words, they are experiences of suffering common to many ordinary people. These conditions affect a significant portion of those who live in our cities and towns. Recent statistics suggest that about 3 in 10 people seek treatment for depression. Drug-based treatment for anxiety is a multibillion dollar business, as is the treatment for other common forms of addiction. Just as physical limitations or injuries are inevitable at some point for most of us, so too mental afflictions may visit us from time to time. These states don't belong only to some less-deserving group, they are widespread and, while their acceptance is growing, these psychological afflictions are generally unwelcomed and thought of in the same way that physical disabilites were 100 years ago. When we walk in the built world, we find that there are very few places or buildings that symbolize or consciously incorporate psychological suffering, places where, for example, the emotionally wounded can find comfort or the isolated and lonely can be acknowledged and welcomed. The homeless and the mentally suffering live in conditions that we all recognize as terrible. Those who are less physically able are obviously not less-deserving human beings, but we have built a world that declares this message loudly and clearly. We did not have to explicitly write an abusive edict to articulate it; the built world is a physical, three-dimensional language that speaks for itself.

Because the built world has always mirrored humankind, the question is: How do we build a world that includes a more compassionate relationship with the unwanted aspects of the self?

From a psychological perspective, the remedy for the built world is that it needs to acquire a new design ability, one that allows us to incorporate the shadow. Even schools, the places where we go to learn about equality and compassion, were not only inaccessible, but their appearance had come to represent places of production and banality. The decision to incorporate into architecture the needs of those who suffer physically and mentally is not only an awakening of compassion, it is a transforming initiation for the imagination of the designer. We have been freed up to begin imagining an imperfect world. This is the new built world that is consciously trying to integrate and recover those aspects that have been ignored and rejected.

The world seems to be witnessing the emergence of the reality of the shadow. From Wall Street to the highest levels of government, from the kitchen in every home to the churches in every community, centuries of power and perfectionism are being challenged by the emergence of the shadow. Harmful or careless acts, events and decisions long concealed by those who enjoyed positions of authority, seem to be coming to light no matter how deeply they have been buried or how much we may wish for them not to appear. It often seems as though there is some autonomous force causing these stories to surface, and in a sense there is, for the dynamic of the shadow obeys a profound law of nature. The universe wants growth. And I hope that we will soon see the value of letting the shadow teach us what we need to learn.

We have been slow to face the reality of the shadow in the built world, but psychology shows us that a strategy of avoidance is dangerous and actually futile. What would happen if designers of the built world undertook the challenge of consciously expressing our shadow aspects? What might our cities look like if we integrated our imperfections? I don't know, but they would reflect a more humane and tolerant view of our humanity and probably embrace those who now feel excluded. The reality is that the shadow is being projected and built now without consciousness, with often brutal and counterintuitive results. When we don't make contact with those states that haunt us and mark us, we are left with a world that does not seem real because it is not dealing with our own psychological reality. The built world becomes detached from us and literally rises above the concerns of most human beings. What we don't recognize, we cannot heal. What hope is there for the built world when we ignore our own nature?

Architecture is no stranger to physical shadow, a condition in which shade is cast by the interception of light. It is widely understood that "darkening" has always been part of the design palette. Shadow is exalted in the reveal, a type of construction detail in which a joint or seam between materials is hidden by recessing a surface. The reveal hides by casting a shadow. A similar idea can be found in the *scotia*–a Greek term for shadow–a concave molding that casts a strong shadow at the base of a column. Its effect is to allow the column to appear to float by obscuring its connection with the ground.

Architecturally, the use of shadow is as powerful as light itself, and these two are obviously in dialogue. At the start of a performance, a darkened room is aroused by a spot of light. Often, at the point of entry to a religious building, we meet a shadowy space before moving through to an expansion of well-lit space. The darkening of a space helps to create a kind of compression before progressing into a sense of expansion accompanied by light. Physical shadow can also make an interior seem unwelcoming or frightening. Horror films are drawn to climax in dark basements and shadowy attics and there are whole parts of cities in which shadowy things are known to occur in contrast to the bright city lights.

According to Rudolph Otto, darkness in our religious buildings, along with silence and emptiness, is necessary to create the physical container for a sense of holiness. The darkness of narrow streets provides the context for the unexpected emergence into bright, sunny, public space. A dramatic indication of our modern refusal to consider the meaning of the shadow is found in the exaggerated level of lighting that now fills our cities and shopping environments. While issues of safety and merchandising drive some of these lighting levels, our cities remain unsafe because our own psychological shadow isn't factored into place making. We are afraid of our own darkness. Annihilating the shadow paradoxically means there can be no sense of security. We need to get to know the reality of our psychological shadow to bring real life and light to our cities.

DESIGNER'S SELF-KNOWLEDGE

Take a few deep breaths and let yourself settle in comfortably.

Read each phrase carefully and allow yourself to spontaneously complete the sentence. If necessary allow several completed sentences to flow from a single phrase. Remember there is no "right" or "wrong" answer. When you feel you have finished a sentence move on to the next one.

When I start a project I feel _____

What I like most about the design process is _____

If I trusted my creativity more _____

My greatest strength is my ability to _____

The most difficult part of designing for me is _____

I get lost when _____

My creativity is _____

If I were more confident _____

Missing from my work is often _____

If I worried less my creativity would _____

For me the process of design is like _____

Right now I need to concentrate on _____

What frustrates me most during the process of design is ____

My project needs more _____

My project needs less _____

I am most confident when _____

Working with others brings out my _____

When I present my work _____

My greatest gift is _____

When you have finished answering these questions you may want to share the results with a friend. The following exercise completes the Designer's Self-Knowledge exercise.

The House of Shadows

Draw an image of a house that contains both the positive and negative traits that have been expressed in the self test. Use the house and its setting to spontaneously create an image or series of images that bring difficulties and talents into one symbolic house. Remember to share the final "design" with a friend, teacher, or counselor.

The Built World as a Barometer of Wholeness

Considering that the evil of our day puts everything that has ever agonized mankind in the deepest shade, one must ask oneself how it is that, for all our progress in the administration of justice, in medicine and in technology, for all our concern with life and health, monstrous engines of destruction have been invented which could easily exterminate the human race.

–C.G. JUNG

Our cities cast a psychological shadow, as do our governments and institutions. These shadow elements manifest in built form the unacceptable and unacknowledged aspects of their collective cultures. We need only look at what we overvalue to see what has been left out. A society that overvalues efficiency loses touch with beauty. A city that single-mindedly puts thinking ahead of feeling is empty and ugly because the places where people can gather are going to be less valued.

The long line of commuters in traffic represent an unconscious reluctance to arrive at jobs we don't like and to return home to relationships we don't enjoy. Would traffic be less of a problem if we were more conscious of our personal needs and desires? Everyone who can recall their dreams has probably experienced a part of a city that is the setting for a narrative filled with anxiety, violence, or despair.

I feel particularly aware of places that are plainly counterintuitive, places where water, earth, and air are toxic. These places have a conscious and unconscious impact on us. Why are such basic ingredients of life so undervalued? These places always leave me feeling drained and defeated about our relationship to life. They

reveal that we may be more split and less perfect then we acknowledge. Yet they are accurate reflections of our collective wellbeing
and our decision making. They are the places that reveal the built
shadow. Our built wasteland is the negative shadow materialized.
We have projected our own unwanted aspects into matter. If we
don't like our own nature, we certainly won't take care of the natural world. If we are lost, then the moraine will be lost. If our ground
water is toxic, we must ask if our own inspiration needs purification. If species are being thoughtlessly eliminated, then it may
signal that our own instinctual energies are being lost.

It is liberating to imagine an architecture that includes a richer
and more complex expression of our inner reality. The modern age
has given us a world with two shadows: one visible, and the other
invisible and felt and trying to bring us down to earth–into our
humanity, to accept our imperfections so that we can become
whole. The psychological shadow of architecture interests me
precisely because it is unconscious. It operates insidiously. We have
developed so much more expertise and been more comfortable
implementing function than incorporating the shadow aspects of
the built world because we often can't see beyond our reliance on
rational thinking. We would much rather concern ourselves with
questions of function and technology then the intensely paradoxical condition of cities founded on waterways that are now toxic.

To paraphrase hypnotherapy's Milton Erickson, we may
consciously want to end homelessness, but unconsciously, we
would rather not confront the issue. On the other hand, we may
consciously decide not to deal with the issue, but unconsciously we
may not want to end homelessness. Both the conscious and the
unconscious minds are involved in the decisions that go into
design. We need to get to know them and bring their dialogue to
our design process. Their complementary partnership is crucial to
our capacity to imagine, desire outcomes, and state intentions. If
we were truly at home with ourselves as individuals, then as a society we would be able to face the challenge of homelessness collectively. We would be more generous because we could relate the
pain and suffering of having nowhere to live and to the more
universal and difficult feeling of not belonging.

We are driven to perfection to avoid our own shadows and we would rather declare war on homelessness then spend time getting to know our own sense of loneliness and alienation. Because we cannot contain what is unloved inside us, we project it onto others –if we happen to be designers, we will project the shadow into artifacts, places, and buildings. We unconsciously use and misdirect our energy to ignore what is disturbing us.

As we have discussed in connection to the creative process, learning how to relate and respond more directly to the true feelings inside us affects what we build. But the outcome of our work is not static. As Jung said, "What we are unconscious of will happen to us as fate." In other words, the aspects of ourselves that we ignore will find a way to become a focus for our attention. The benefit of integrating the shadow is that we will have a more humane and emotionally honest world. The strength of the world will be more than its power, it will be in its willingness to not use power over others to feel comfortable.

An important message of shadow work is to design with humility. It's often the secret ingredient of a creative project, allowing us to acknowledge that we still have something to learn. It is difficult to receive an inspiration if you believe you know exactly what is right. The shadow is always ready to bring us down to earth.

The New Public Space of Shadows

> When the blackest aspects of the shadow, the most negative features of one's life and fate, are seen in relation to one's total life destiny, they change their character. They become acceptable and a meaningful part of the whole.
> –E. EDINGER

Human settlement has always included public space. Places to gather, to celebrate military victory, exchange goods, share religious beliefs, or spontaneously meet friends are a part of our collective civic inheritance and have been evolving for centuries. The character of these public spaces can take many forms. London is identified with its many squares, Paris was transformed by its great boulevards, Venice's canals have inspired artists as diverse as

Caneletto and Thomas Mann. The diverse ways in which public space give cities their abiding character and identity remains a unique testament to human creativity.

EXERCISE

The following visualization exercises are intended to help you access a more "shadowful design," the architecture for an imperfect world, a world where there is suffering. These exercises are intended for reflection and to encourage you to draw from your own experience of imperfection.

When I say imagine, I am asking you to look inward and allow an image as symbol to come to consciousness that you can transcribe into a drawing. Begin this exercise by relaxing and after each image return to your natural relaxed state and take a few breaths to refresh yourself. Remember to check in with your body. There is no need to rush.

Imagine a real dream house, a house for dreaming.
Imagine a public place where those who feel defeated can rest.
Imagine a house where the emotionally wounded feel comforted.
Imagine an imperfect building, one that expresses the difficulty of living.
Imagine a door to your own shadow.
Imagine a house where everyone is encouraged to slow down.
Imagine a room that encourages listening.
Imagine a landscape that welcomes those who feel anxious.

Imagine a facade that can't hold things together.
Imagine a public space for giving thanks.
Imagine the house where your shadow lives.
Imagine a house where peace talks might be held.
Imagine an urban place for those who find the loss of nature intolerable.

Imagine a door that will never open.
Imagine a place in the city that celebrates the discovery of the unconscious. Where in your city does such a place belong?
Imagine a public space where those who are separated come together.
Imagine a public garden that protests violence.

Imagine the elevation of a school that teaches listening.
Imagine a table that accepts and holds conversations about
    suffering and imperfection.
Imagine an elevation that brings to our attention the loss of forests,
    species, and fresh water.

Design a garden that allows us to suffer our loneliness.
Design a public space for those who have assimilated their shadow.
    What would such a public space look like and what would it mean
    to its citizens?

The Shrine

Long ago every home had a kind of shrine. A place where the world was reconciled and the dynamics of the universe were alive. Imagine a shrine, a holy place that can hold the suffering of the world. A place where the victims of attack or the long ignored are acknowledged and recognized. An altar for the suffering of the world. This is a place we need to acknowledge because it symbolizes a place we all have to visit from to time to time. Where in your home would you locate this place? Where in the place you work does this place belong? Remember this shrine can change with the seasons or events of your life to express the connection between your inner world and built world.

Imagine a place, a room or landscape for those who feel gripped by
    fear, anxiety, and uncertainty.
Imagine a public space that addresses a violent world.
Imagine a space of reconciliation in your city. What is the first and most
    important quality or artifact of this place? Can you sit in the place?
    What are its qualities?

I hope these exercises begin to bring the wisdom and creativity of the shadow into your work. They grow out of the thought that whatever we are capable of experiencing we can and will express through built form. It may seem strange to suggest that states of suffering that we might otherwise reject or ignore be built, but we have to remember that these states are most dangerous when we fail to recognize them and build them unconsciously. This is a call for all of us to consciously include them in our design practices. If we are successful, we may be able to turn a liability into a creative experience we can learn from.

Maya Lyn, The Viet Nam Memorial

This project brought into the world a modern way of making contact with the shadow. War is by definition destructive, but the Viet Nam War was a conflict that sent waves of division right through the American psyche. It divided nations, communities, and families. It left us shaken because it challenged our very definitions of victory and defeat. When the time came to establish some kind of memorial to this war, the demands placed on the design were as fraught as the experience of the war itself. Of necessity, the Viet Nam memorial required a space and symbol that could safely contain many different kinds of anguish. It could be not a war monument that celebrated victory, but a monument that could contain healing. For the American people to find closure, there would need to be acceptance of the complex of experiences of the whole psyche. And it could not simply honor the nationalism or the special adrenaline of war but offer a place to reflect on conflict and seek resolution. Who would visit this place? Curious Americans. Families–brothers, sisters, mothers, fathers, cousins, friends, and colleagues–touched directly or indirectly by loss and by shades of conflict. This monument had to declare and shelter a position that could include all who have been touched by the memories and actions of war. It needed to be able to hold this sad, angry array of emotions for future generations.

The site for the Viet Nam Memorial is a special part of Washington, DC: the Mall. The Mall is an attempt to formalize the essence of America, what the built world would look like if it were the American ideal. The Mall is about perfection, or at least about the possibility of a perfect country, in which every individual is an ambitious yet thoughtful self-governing citizen whose voice can be heard through free speech and the vote, a country blessed with natural wealth and robust energy. The Mall is a unified geometric campus of supremely confident white neo-classical buildings. There have been slight exceptions made, such as the aerospace museum, but even these exceptions are in the spirit of neoclassicism; they embody an ideal. Every monument repeats the ritual of rising up to the interior as though the visitor was entering a temple. They are all symmetrical, and the grand moment of entry is carried internally into a large rotunda that contains white marble representations from the pantheon of great leaders. These places are built instructions, an invitation to emulate, celebrate, and follow the example. Who knows or really has time to ask if we are still so confident or excited about declaring what we stand for? Who is going to dare question these powerful symbols we aspire to become? This area of Washington is a living symbol and the spiritual center of the United States.

Entering the Viet Nam Memorial

We go down to it. Down is to modernity what the Pacific Ocean was to the age of exploration: our last, eternal frontier, the last great unknown. The monument is everywhere and we can barely summon the courage to look at it, let alone set out to explore it. But journey down we must because everything except the great deep spaces that go down forever inside us has already been discovered. We know instinctively that once we descend, we can never again rise as innocently into the sweet blue sky. We go down into earth, where trenches and graves are dug and battles are fought. With a shimmering dark wall beside our path, we find that we suddenly want to go down.

We need to know about the going down—not just the direction, but also the experience of descent. Are you aware of the act of giving up the possibility of all other directions? There will be no going up and out, we are heading down and when we go down, we are inevitably going in. There are names to read and the names on a war monument are death. Death is spoken here—it's heavy—and we're beginning to go down. We have forgotten that this trip to below the horizon is temporary. Once you begin to go down, a strange familiarity creeps in us. The sky is still blue overhead, the possibility for courage is with us. We are not alone; this is, after all, the Mall in Washington. This is the center of the power of the brave and the home of the free. We all go down into the great black box of memory, together, down into the night of remembering. We descend slowly, the world collapsing into the dark wall beside us. And we continue to sink down. The act of descending is taking us into matter. Lessons rise up inside us when we consciously go down. Knees bend and are stressed differently; the entire body is registering a small cry. We descend and we loosen. This is not a winding trail, but a straight line cut in the ceremonial ground. This was never meant as a graveyard, but it is often how we ultimately understand the idea of entering the earth. The earth is our last virgin frontier. We are all going down to visit the ground of our being.

My father grew up in a city, but he is buried in a suburban ceme-
tery. A stone gives his name and dates. The physical place has no
meaning or memories and I seldom visit–the place is not worth a
pilgrimage and seems no more than a business arrangement. I can
just as easily imagine him anywhere. But it makes no sense to me
that his life ends in this empty suburban cemetery, where there was
no effort to construct a setting that has meaning. This is what we
do now. Death has become a business transaction and a private
affair. I travel to the suburban grave with my own memories that
the world cannot mirror. When my father was lowered into the
earth, I felt myself raised.

We are going to visit the inside of the monument, the great unconscious, the vast ocean of mysterious, unknown things. Black walls reflect sorrow back to us more brightly than we expect. We are turning dark while the day stays bright. We have dropped below the normal level of the perfect and powerful city. The noise is gone, the monuments are gone, and the white statues are gone. The news and current events that make this city important are gone. It's not like those other places. This is a beautiful place of difficulty. We are safely contained within a roaring memory. Many people experience meaning here and must leave something at this wall. It gives us something so freely and generously that we want to give something back. The climb up and out is a relief–the air is sweeter, and we breathe a little deeper and appreciate our lives.

PART FOUR

Inner Know-How

This chapter explores many of the tools that are already used by designers and architects. What makes them significant for the inner studio is that while most of them are well known, they are usually self-taught or developed through self-exploration and they are very rarely discussed. By becoming more aware of the way these practices work and how they can help us, I hope to be able to enhance the creative abilities of designers.

Visualization

Designers walk through the buildings they design long before they are built, crossing bridges, standing on streets, enjoying rooms and gardens long before clients give their approval for construction to begin. And all of this happens effortlessly without them ever having to leave the comfort of their favorite chairs.

The designer's capacity to create and manipulate pictures in the mind's eye is developed through the practice of visualization. It is a very useful design tool because it provides a completely friction-free environment in which we can directly interact with our imagination. What is most remarkable about visualization is not what it allows us to do, but that it remains largely self-taught. Although most designers are aware of visualization and use it regularly, we are rarely given an opportunity to develop this skill consciously. A more mindful enhancement of visualization can become a cornerstone of the design development process. After exploring visualization, we will move into the practice of active imagination, which allows us to extend the depth and breadth of visualization by increasing the role of the unconscious in imagination.

Many designers are visually oriented and find visualization a very natural thing to do. Ask designers a question about the built world and they automatically "see" their answers. As they begin to describe their responses, they are actually describing the images they have "seen" or in some way "sensed" internally. Designers don't do this because they are taught to, but because this is how our minds work. Forming images is a crucial mechanism in the process of thinking and people who are visually inclined are more likely to "see" their thinking—albeit unconsciously.

As we shall see, visualization is not just the capacity to see objects in the mind's eye—it may include hearing, sensing, touching, or tasting, or any combination of these vehicles of perception. The key is to get to know which of these avenues works best for you.

In the inner studio, visualization means learning to consciously work with images as they are created in the mind's eye. We want to become skillful at not only "picturing" the places and things we are trying to make, but also more practiced at summoning the subtle levels of feeling that are responsible for our own internal image making. We want to bring the rich and complex world of the imagination into the making of our world.

Drawing or modeling visualized images means capturing the essence of the image—adding details and all manner of elaboration make up the content of the development phase of design. The drawing has to carry enough information to allow the image to unfold and to allow us access back to the visualization. The act of drawing or modeling is an essential element of the design process because it connects us with the process of materializing the image. I will discuss this further after exploring the inner world of imagination first through visualization and then through active imagination.

The Experience of Visualization

When we observe an image in the mind's eye, we see the images within; our eyes don't have to be open. What distinguishes visualization from active imagination is that visualization works when we know what we want to visualize and directs the unconscious to produce the image. We already have an image, perhaps a memory, texture, or condition, and want to put our sense of what is best to the test.

When we draw something, we are often not aware that we have actually recorded what we first saw in the mind's eye. And what we saw first in the mind's eye was in turn prompted by subtle thoughts and messages that occurred below the threshold of consciousness. It's this closely packed and mentally automatic process that we want to get hold of and begin to develop more consciously.

Our brain is typically operating in what are called beta waves. Experiments in psycho-immunology have determined that in order to optimize visualization, we need to access alpha waves. Alpha waves allow us to remember more, think more clearly, and find creative solutions more easily. The key to accessing this state is relaxation. Daydreaming, reverie, brainstorming, and active imagination are all part of the same family of visualizing processes that are enhanced through relaxation. All of these practices have great usefulness in developing the faculty of imagination in the process of architectural design. The modern designer has to be able to not only to access these states, but also get to know the felt sense of these practices.

Preliminary Practices

"Start the way you mean to go on."
–Anonymous

In the practice of visualization, it's important to remember that our starting point is critical to our outcome. Our first step is to set an intention, beginning with reflecting on the purpose of the project. You are letting the depth–your unconscious–know what you are intending. This can range from "I want to design a house" to "May this house be a place of joy and peace." The intention for a street may be to connect strangers or to create a place where people walk in beauty.

After establishing an intention, we prepare ourselves for relaxing by connecting with our bodies. The simplest way to do this is to ask yourself how you are feeling, right now, in the present. How does your body feel? Listen for the body's response, which is usually a felt response and signal to release or to soften. Acknowledge this, letting your shoulders drop, or taking a deep breath, filling your lungs, then exhaling, setting free any tension. We want to consciously prepare to receive something new.

Over time this step of setting an intention, followed by relaxation, can be accomplished in seconds, but in the beginning it's important to make sure that you have gone through these steps fully and consciously. It's helpful to get to know the feeling of the right intention and the right mind-body state. In the world of visualization, attention is energy. What you put before your mind's eye will gather energy. And what is unconsciously before your mind's eye will also gather energy. Too much effort and nothing will be received. Too much relaxation and nothing will matter. Finding a balance between these two points is the art of visualization.

EXERCISE: EXPLORING YOUR ABILITY TO VISUALIZE

The following visualization exercises are intended to take you into the inner studio. The first exercise is designed to acquaint you with your existing skills and develop your awareness of the potential of visualization. Remember not to force your experience, but to allow the suggestions to find their most natural response. Try to simply be a witness to the experiences and images that arise in your mind's eye. After stretching, begin by getting comfortable in your chair. Loosen any tight clothing, feel free to remove your glasses and remember that everyone has their own way of becoming comfortable—there is no right or wrong way. Become aware of your breathing, inhaling and exhaling normally. As you continue to breathe naturally, evenly and easily, let each inhalation be refreshing and allow the exhalation to be a relaxed letting go. Remember there is no need to force anything, if an image does not come to mind easily, simply return to your breathing. After a few breaths, gently try again. If you find yourself getting tense or getting a headache, stop and take a break. In the beginning, short sessions are best and these can be extended as you discover what works best for you. Allow the chair or floor to take the full weight of your body. Let any tightness or holding you feel in your body to release. As I ask you to imagine a variety of things, observe what happens to you. Notice any sensations or images that occur to you.

1. Now imagine a blue circle. You may imagine it on a screen like a TV or computer screen or you may see it in your mind's eye. Notice the size of the circle. Is it large or small? Notice if the color is vivid and clear. Is there more than one blue circle? Remembering to breath easily...Does the circle change as you watch it? If you would like to change the blue circle, imagine that you have a full set of controls like those on a computer or TV and go ahead and adjust the circle so that it looks the way you want it to look. Remember to breathe normally as you observe the circle that you have created. When you are ready, allow the circle to become a very spacious blue sphere floating lightly and easily. Just take a moment to observe this....

2. On the next exhalation, let the image fade away and create in your mind's eye a red triangle. Notice the color–is it bright red? Is it large or small? Are the edges clear? Use your ability to control the image until the triangle becomes steady. Remember to enjoy a relaxed attitude, inhaling and exhaling normally as you see the red triangle becoming a pyramid, and allow it to slowly rotate. Does the pyramid seem to be above you or below you?

3. Now let that image fade and begin to image a yellow square. Feel free to experiment with its size. As you continue, relaxed and comfortable, imagine that the yellow square becomes a three-dimensional cube that becomes transparent. Remember to let the weight of your body settle into the chair or floor. Let yourself see the blue sphere and the red triangle appear inside the yellow cube. Just see them floating there. Take a moment to play with the way these objects can interact in your mind's eye.

4. Now imagine that you are standing in front of a very large door. It appears very thick and heavy with massive hinges and a dark wooden texture. You reach for the golden handle and are surprised when the door glides opens so easily. Remembering to breath in a relaxed way, you enter and are now standing in a tall round space with light streaming in through a tall window. A fire is burning in the fireplace and the room is very quiet. Your desk and chair are there, near a window. You know you can easily work here.

5. Now let that image fade away, and imagine that you are walking along a beautiful beach with the sun warming your body. You can

feel the warmth of the sand on your feet as you walk along the beach. As you near the water's edge, you begin to enjoy the soothing, rhythmic sound of the waves. Standing where the surf and sand meet you can feel your feet cooled by the smooth waves as they pull sand from around your feet. Take a moment to enjoy the sensations on the beach....

6. Now continue to feel comfortable as that fantasy fades and imagine you are walking home on a bright winter's day, down a country road. Your body is warm inside your thick winter coat, and you can clearly see your breath with each exhalation. In the distance there is a house with smoke rising from the chimney. A black crow is calling out through the bright winter air. When you reach your house, you climb three steps and stand at the wooden door where you can smell the aroma of coffee.

7. Now imagine yourself in the country walking through the forest on a beautiful summer day. The path is well-marked, and the air is refreshing. Sunlight pours through the forest canopy, lighting wild mushrooms and flowers near the path. This is a peaceful place. You see a clearing in the distance and you decide to sit there on an old log. The place feels very alive and you feel very connected to nature. Centered... grounded...and confident. Notice how your body feels. Breathing normally, imagine a peaceful light radiating from inside you. Just let that feeling radiate outward until it fills your whole body.

8. Now let this fantasy fade. Return to this room, and let yourself take a few deep breaths. When you are ready, stretch and become alert. Take a moment to remember your experiences and begin to write out the important or noteworthy moments. Take as much time as you need to record your experiences. And when you have finished writing, discuss the experiences with a friend.

This exercise takes you through an experience of imagining using your five senses. It can help you to discover your particular gifts of imagination. We all have our favorite way to imagine things–some of us are more attuned to seeing things, for others the sense of touch or sound or smell may dominate. There are no right or wrong visualizations. Were the colors you imagined vivid or were you more able to hear church bells? Could you smell of the roses or were you surprised by who you met in the forest? Try to discover your dominant sense and experiment with bringing it into your create work. Experiment with your capacity for visualization and find out which of your senses is easiest to connect with and which is least developed.

EXERCISE

The following visualization can help you prepare yourself to dwell in a creative inner environment.

Begin by taking a few deep breaths. Check in with your body and allow your jaw and shoulders to soften. With each exhalation, allow your body to settle into whatever surface is supporting it. There is no work to do...just let go and relax as you continue to breathe peacefully. Now imagine that you are in beautiful garden on a lovely summer morning. There is a large hot tub beneath the trees and you decide to relax in the warm water. Settle slowly into the water until your body is immersed in soothing warm water...all stress and worry leave your body...the water covers your shoulders...only your head is in the bright summer air. With each exhalation you become aware of how relaxed your body feels while your mind remains open and quiet. Enjoy the images that bubble up through your mind's eye. Open to the wonderful breezes that move through the tall trees...relax and allow yourself to review things from a new angle.

This is a wonderful environment for imagining design, where it is possible to visualize your work and pay attention to the physiological fallout of images. Remember that if your thinking is too critical or too tight, you may need to spend more time relaxing your body in order to receive images. If you are too relaxed, you won't notice or care about what is being visualized. So along with this relaxed body, you need to have an alert yet peaceful mind. Maintaining these two conditions takes practice, but the goal is to be nicely balanced, at ease and awake at the same time. The deeper and more open the relaxation, the more freely images can move through your mind. A relaxed environment is ideal for creating; any creative work will thrive in this atmosphere.

EXERCISE: PROMPTING THE VISUALIZATION

Remember to have paper and pencils ready. In the beginning, drawing and visualization may seem like two very different practices, but in time you will find that it is possible and effortless to bring these two activities together. If you are experienced, you can begin directly with the project you are working on. Beginners may want to practice visualizing a favorite place, a place that has a healing quality, or a safe place that you really find peaceful. It may be your secret sanctuary in the city or the forest, it may be on a beach or in a special room.

Close your eyes and begin by thinking about the place and watching for an image in your mind's eye. You may think of one thing, but the image that arises may be different. Try experimenting with different internal directions to get a feeling for the kinds of inner directions that are most effective for you. Direct the visualization to follow what you are curious about. If you enjoy the way light is falling into the space you are imagining, make an image of that phenomenon. These drawings are copies of what we see in the mind's eye. The drawing may depart from the visualization, just as the visualization may have departed from your first image. Go with your creative instincts and follow the images inspired by your imagination. It is really impossible to draw anything without first seeing this image or having a felt sense of it. In fact, it probably isn't helpful to draw at all if no images are forthcoming. Some people enjoy the act of drawing and create this way, but behind the movement of the pen, mental images are guiding what appears on the page.

It's helpful to get the feel of playing with images in your mind's eye to shift your attention to the images and pictures in your mind. It's a process whereby you allow images to float and move through your mind's eye as if you were watching a school of fish swim by. If you see something that moves you, you might choose to look at it more closely. When you feel yourself losing interest in an image and your concentration wavers, let it go–whether it is a drawing or an internal image. The beginning stage is not the time to fight through. Instead, return to the intention of the exercise you began with.

We want to take advantage of internal states of imagination, which are free of many of the worldly restrictions a design project will eventually encounter. With your eyes slightly closed, there are no problems with budget, there are no physical constraints of the site–you are completely free to tune into your imagination. This approach acknowledges that we usually draw what we have already visualized, but the process may occur so quickly that we are not aware of the step of visualizing. Now we want to not only be aware of this step, but to use its frictionless quality to let the imagination roam, churn, and play. The creation of images is a delicate business. It's like observing a wild animal—they may be more willing to arrive if they do not sense fear or sharp scrutiny. This way of working allows the architect or designer to play the role of alchemist or conjurer, developing a relationship with the external world in the imagination.

In the curriculum for the inner studio, you would spend as much time practicing visualization as developing a knowledge of structure and cultural history.

You can begin to practice visualization by simply remembering a place you have been. Start with a place that you like. The goal is to picture the place in your mind's eye and simply "review" it your memory. This image may be bright or dull, it may be stationary or full of sound and movement. Your goal is to make contact with the image. We naturally bring to design an extensive library of experiences in the form of images. Visualization may involve recollecting these stored artifacts and experiences or creating entirely new images.

As we design we are generating images and it quickly becomes possible through visualization to allow the world of stored images and the world of new speculations to mingle, and to use these new images to prompt, answer, and test design speculations, ideas, and instincts. This visualization is really a very agile, very provisional tool. In the blink of an eye, we can rotate a building, change its color, or revise an entry sequence. We can work with variations that are either very detailed or on the scale of a city.

EXERCISE: PRACTICING VISUALIZATION

Another level of visualization involves holding an image in your mind's eye while at the same time tuning into your body. For example, imagine the room you work in. Visualize the room, see yourself in the room, and then bring your attention to your body for a kinesthetic response. Does your body feel strong or weak? Tune into the subtle level of feeling provoked by the image held in your mind. Try this exercise with rooms of different shapes and colors you are designing. Remember not to force the visualization. Allow it to arise naturally and bring your awareness to the sensations in your body. Using the picture in the mind's eye, we can learn from the kinesthetic knowing of the body.

If you are trying to choose a particular detail or artifact and need additional feedback, you can use visualization to gain information about your choice. In your mind's eye, imagine either holding or touching whatever it is your choice concerns and pay close attention to the sensations in your body. It's important to see your hand resting on the wooden window frame or the aluminum chair, or whatever it is you are visualizing, and feel the texture of the material in your hand.

If you are sketching or constructing a model, it's often helpful to test the creative proposition in the mind's eye. Picture the outcome inwardly as you create outwardly. With experience, visualization becomes a kind of combination of inner guidance and creative shorthand. The mind has immense processing and picturing capabilities, and design is a wonderful opportunity to develop them. I find that most people really enjoy the friction-free atmosphere of visualization. It is only necessary to see the image for a moment; to sustain a steady visualization will take longer. The goal when we start out is to discover what works best for us. Which tools and which rhythms of creative work are most helpful to you?

Active Imagination

Without this playing with fantasy no creative work has ever yet come to birth. The debt we owe to the play of imagination is incalculable.
–C.G. JUNG

Carl Jung saw that the unconscious was the great source for images and symbol making. Through his own psychological searching, he developed a technique that allowed the conscious mind access to the unconscious mind. He called this technique "active imagination," a modern name for something that has been practiced in different forms for centuries. Its purpose is to get in touch with what the unconscious mind wants to say. We can use this at the start of a project when we are looking for an inspiration, a deeper seed from which to grow a project. Or we may wish to use this technique any time we find ourselves searching for a fresh perspective or solution to a design problem. It may take the form of a written exercise, movement of the body, exploring the voice, painting, or sculpting. It can be developed through images first encountered in a dream or from a feeling in the body. Its essence rests on a capacity to facilitate communication between conscious and unconscious aspects of the psyche.

What makes active imagination so valuable to the designer is that it mimics the inner activity that accompanies the act of design. Active imagination is intended to bring awareness to the inner dynamic of design. The key is a sincere desire to learn what the unconscious has to offer. There is no effort to control the content; the only requirement is to record faithfully the expression of whatever arises from within. The place where the creative begins is internal; it's the place where the mind's essential clarity manifests.

You are learning to recognize and track the subtle inner voices and images of the unconscious. This is a process that delights in the unpredictable richness of the imagination. It is an active celebration of the power of expression, where words and images are free of all responsibilities. The only necessity is that these impulses be retrieved from the underworld–or from whatever corner of the body or mind they were born in–and honestly recorded.

Guided Imagery Exercises

The next exercise is a protocol for relaxing before beginning the experience of active imagination. The second exercise introduces you to a specific way to deepen this practice. The third exercise presents a framework for getting answers to any questions you may have. The fourth exercise introduces you to the possibility of deepening your work by connecting with your body. The final exercise explores inspiration and is probably most helpful after you have gained some experience and comfort with guided imagery.

You can work through any of these exercises by reading them to yourself, but they will be more effective if you have a friend with a pleasant voice read them aloud so that you are free to concentrate on your own responses. You may also want to record yourself reading these scripts and then use the recording to work through the exercises.

It is important that you keep a notebook and pen nearby so you can record your experiences after each exercise. When you start out, make sure you will not be interrupted during an exercise and allow time for your own de-briefing. This has several levels, beginning with recording your experience in a journal, notebook, or sketchbook, and includes discussing the experience with a trusted friend, teacher, or counselor. These steps are very important because the contents of an active imagination need to be integrated. The sharing of these inner experiences allows us to see and hear the products of the unconscious from a more objective and ego-centered point of view. This step needs to be understood as the completion of the exercise and is as important as any other moment in the active imagination process. After many years of experience, these protocols may become less structured, but they remain most effective when approached with patience, reverence, and care. This is very important to remember when we work with images from the unconscious.

EXERCISE 1: PROGRESSIVE RELAXATION

Relaxation can be learned; regular practice will improve your skill level and will enable the benefits of this exercise to enter your life. The key is to remember not to force anything. Be gentle with yourself during the process and try to bring a light-hearted, attentive, and curious state of mind to the exercise.

For this exercise, make sure you will not be disturbed for 20 or 30 minutes. Loosen any tight clothing or belts, and perhaps take off your shoes and remove your glasses. Find a comfortable posture and settle in there, remembering to breathe normally. You may sit in a chair or lie on your back on the floor. As you inhale, take in energy; as you exhale, imagine letting go of any tightness and worry you are holding. Let the weight of your body go down into the chair or into the floor. Remember that you can change your posture when you need to. Let the sensation of breathing, inhaling and exhaling normally, fill your body with peaceful energy.

Become aware of the sensation of your right foot making contact with the floor and allow the weight of your right foot to go down into the floor with each exhalation. Just let go of any tension or holding or discomfort in your right foot and ankle with each exhalation. Allow a softening and ease to come to your right foot.

When you are ready, with another inhalation, become aware of your left foot. Just become aware of the way it rests on the floor and let any unnecessary holding go down into the floor. Let any tightness drop away as you continue to breathe normally. Let the weight of your left ankle go into the floor, and feel the warmth of your foot.

When you are ready, bring your awareness to your right calf and begin to allow the first sensations of tightness to release, inhaling and exhaling with normally relaxed breathing. Remember all you need to do right now is use your mind to let go of any holding in your right calf.

And now bring your attention to your left calf and imagine you are inhaling and exhaling from your left calf. With each exhalation, allow your left calf to soften and relax. There is no special work to do now as you experience the letting go in your left calf.

Inhaling and exhaling normally, see if you can feel a sensation of comfort and relaxation warming and spreading through your legs so that your right thigh relaxes and feels more comfortable on the chair. Bring your attention to your left thigh and allow it to settle even more comfortably on the chair. As you do so, you may take a moment to experience a growing ease and comfort as you inhale and exhale normally. Remember that it is quite possible to adjust your posture whenever you need to get more comfortable. Listen to your body.

As you do so, bring your attention to your lower back and buttocks area and allow a feeling of relaxation to expand and soften this hard-working area of your body. With each exhalation, let all the weight and holding of your lower body to soften and lighten. You can use your mind to let go by gently bringing your attention to your lower back and buttocks.

Now allow your abdomen to soften, bringing your awareness to your belly and stomach. Allow all the organs of your abdomen to relax as you continue to breathe normally, inhaling and exhaling, enjoying all the new ways you are experiencing learning about the relaxed sensations in your body.

Now bring your breathing and awareness to your right shoulder and, as you inhale and exhale normally, let your right shoulder release, remembering, if you are right-handed, all the drawing and computer work done with the right arm and hand. Breathe into the right hand and arm and, with your next exhalation, let go of any holding or stress. Use this moment to feel the weight of your right arm and hand as it rests more comfortably.

When you are ready, bring your attention to your left shoulder. We all shoulder many loads. As you breathe comfortably, bring the sensation of letting go to your left shoulder and let that feeling expand through your left arm, down into your left hand, and down into the sensation of your fingers. Let the weight of the arm go down onto whatever your hand and arm rests upon.

Now take a moment to feel the relaxed, comfortable condition of your body from the shoulders, lower back, buttocks and legs, letting the weight of your body be comfortably supported by the chair. Just take a moment to be. There is no work to do, no assignment or car or bill. Just be with your body in a relaxed moment and see if you can memorize this sensation.

Take a moment to feel the muscles in your neck, the back of your neck, your throat, and your jaw, letting go of any holding. Let your muscles soften with each exhalation. Listen inwardly to the muscles of your neck and jaw as they let go, and as that softness and ease spread into your scalp and forehead, let your eyes relax so that any stress in your neck, jaw, scalp, and eyes softens and your body begins to settle in comfortably. As you continue to breathe easily, take a moment to enjoy and memorize pleasant sensations as you learn new ways to open and relax your body.

Take a moment to scan your body, breathing normally, exhaling and inhaling. Take a moment to be with your relaxed body, see if there are any places that you are drawn to that need softening. Go there now, inhaling and exhaling, letting these places soften and see if there is a lightness, a relaxed, slight feeling of freedom in your body.

When you are ready, on the next inhalation, begin to open your eyes, stretch, or yawn, and as you become more alert, roll to your right side and continuing to relax, gently using your arms to help yourself sit up. Take a moment to write out your experience before sharing it with a friend.

EXERCISE 2: DEEPENING THE EXPERIENCE

This guided active imagination exercise can be used to deepen your experience. As with every exercise it is important to find a time and place where you will not be disturbed and to make sure you share the results with a friend after you have recorded your experience.

Imagine yourself at the top of a staircase. It may be a straight or spiral stair. It may be made of wood, steel, glass, or stone. Take a moment to imagine the stair you are standing on. Observe it in detail, noticing how steep the stairs are, how wide. Feel the railing in your hand. What is the texture beneath your feet? When you are ready, let yourself notice how your body feels as you begin to descend one step at a time. Count backwards from ten to one with each step down the stairs. Experience the feeling of deeper relaxation, breathing normally, inhaling and exhaling, as you go. Feel the railing with your hand and the solid stairs beneath your feet. Ten, nine–comfortably descending; eight, seven, six–easy and unworried. As you reach the fifth step, halfway down the stairs, take a moment to enjoy the comfortable sensation that is growing as you descend. When you are ready, continue your experience. Four, three, two, one–at the bottom of the stairs, become aware of a new space, with its own quality of light, its own feeling.

As you become curious about this place you see a remarkable doorway. Somehow you know that you are meant to go through it. When you are ready, step through the doorway and begin your creative work by asking a question. When you are finished, climb up the stairs counting from 1 to 10 and come back to this time and place refreshed and ready to write out your experience.

EXERCISE 3: THE INNER STUDIO GUIDE

Now imagine yourself in a beautiful place, quiet and serene. It may be in the country or in an ancient city. It may be a place you've always wanted to visit or it may be a place you know from your travels. It doesn't really matter–just allow the image of a very special place to come to you, a place where you feel comfortable, where the light and space combine just the way you like. And now let yourself begin to explore the interior of the place and take a moment to enjoy what it is you see there, the interesting materials and details, the pleasant smells, the temperature, the sounds you can hear–let your body and mind enjoy the physical sensation of being fully immersed in this beauty.

You have the deep feeling that this is an ideal place for you to be creative. And so you take out a sketch book and as you do so, you sense that the most amazing things can happen in this place at this time. You decide to invite someone who has always creatively inspired you to join you in this place. You may or may not have met this person before, but you know that he or she is with you now.

You begin to focus inwardly on a question that is very important to you. What do you ask?

Notice whether a symbol appears.

If you are uncertain about the response, go ahead and ask another question and continue the dialogue until you have learned all that you need to at this time.

Remembering to inhale and exhale normally, use this time to enjoy how your unconscious mind is free to explore the images from different angles or perhaps form new perspectives while your conscious mind participates effortlessly, guiding these new possibilities.

Now take a moment to imagine how your project would develop with the support of your inspiring guide and how your work might change if you put his or her guidance into action.

When you are ready, begin to prepare to return to this room at this time, knowing you can always meet in this way again, whenever you need to.

Now climb back up the stairs–one, two–you are more alert and feeling refreshed–three steps up, four, five–you are waking up with each climbing motion. Six, seven–you are ready to come back to this room–eight, nine, ten–you are breathing comfortably.

And now return, refreshed, ready to learn from your experience. Stretch or yawn and begin to record your fantasy.

EXERCISE 4: ACTIVE IMAGINATION FOR THE BODY

Find a comfortable position and settle in there. Begin to focus on your breathing and, as you do so, enjoy the feeling of relaxation and comfort that registers in your body and mind as you continue to breathe normally.

Now, when you are ready, imagine yourself smiling. It may be a smile like the Mona Lisa's or it may be like Tina Turner's–it doesn't matter how you smile, only that you connect with the sensation of smiling. Take a moment to enjoy this feeling, and allow the sensations of smiling to spread from your mouth and lips into your cheeks and face. Quietly, let yourself be at one with this experience. Notice any softening or warmth or spreading comfort that feels pleasant.

On the next inhalation, bring the sensation of smiling to your eyes. Imagine your eyes and the skin around your eyes softening. Allow your eyes to rest in this generous, loving way–we are usually too busy depending on our eyes to consider how fortunate we are to see so effortlessly. We have been able to see so many beautiful things–loved ones, friends, our favorite places in nature, wonderful art. This exercise gives us the chance to give thanks for all we have seen. Giving thanks to our eyes connects us with giving thanks for all the beauty we have experienced. We have also seen many things that were difficult to take in, that were discordant and difficult. Allow this sense of the smiling in your eyes to remain as you let go of any scenes you may be carrying that need to be acknowledged and released.

On the next inhalation, bring the sensation of the smile to your ears. Imagine your ears softening. We have all been fortunate to hear so many wonderful sounds, the voices of those we love, the sound of birds on a summer morning, our favorite songs, ocean waves. Allow a feeling of gratitude to spread though your ears. With each inhalation and each exhalation, allow yourself to give thanks for the joy of hearing and, with smiling ears, allow yourself to release anything you may have heard that was not pleasant, letting go of harmful voices or aggressive sounds–just allow them to fall away with each exhalation.

Return to the sensation of smiling again and be present with the sensation of your smile. When you are ready, allow your inner smile to settle in your tongue. Let your jaw soften, let the skin inside your mouth relax and give thanks for the simple pleasure of taste. We have all enjoyed the taste of a cool drink on a hot day, a sweet peach–we enjoy so many things and never really think of our good fortune in being able to taste, yet if we lost this sense our world would be less joyful. Allow the inner smile to spread though your mouth, teeth, and tongue, and allow a sense of gratitude to grow. With each exhalation, let go of anything that has disturbed you, anything that was difficult to swallow.

On the next inhalation, bring the inner smile to your nose, allowing your sense of breathing to relax. Our breathing is fundamental to our health and energy–even a short period of congestion causes great discomfort–so appreciate the miracle of our breathing and the great pleasure of smelling the forest or our favorite flowers or fresh-baked pie. Remember as you exhale to let any smell that was not pleasant be released and set free.

Now return to the sensation of smiling and, when you are ready, gently bring the inner smile into your throat, the place where your neck and chest meet, the place where communication comes from. We constantly rely on communication, but rarely are we aware of the wonder and joy of speaking, the fulfilling experience of being able to express ourselves. Allow yourself to give thanks for this wonderful ability. Take a moment to inwardly enjoy the sensation of spreading warmth in the throat area, warmth that comes from breathing in gratitude and releasing any tightness. With your smile in your throat area, allow anything we have said that was harmful to be released–just allow anything negative to be dissolved into the earth without any further judgment

And now, with the next inhalation, bring the inner smile to your heart. Take a moment to memorize the spreading comfort and warmth, and allow this feeling of good energy to fill more and more of your chest, spreading outward into your neck and face and downward into your belly and legs. Allow yourself to be filled with the sensation radiating from your inner smile, from your heart. Use this time to experience the feeling of the inner smile alive in every cell. If you know of someone who needs love and support at this time, see them in your mind's eye smiling, see them happy and in light. Breathing in and breathing out, be with them in this way.

And when you feel you have connected with them, imagine yourself receiving from them the same loving energy. See and really feel yourself receiving their good energy. Spend some time exploring this. If there are others to whom you wish to send this energy, do so now.

When you feel that you are done, bring your attention back to the sensation of your smile. Continue to breathe normally and, when you are ready, return to this room at this time. Open your eyes, stretch, and take a few moments to gently come back alert to this room and time. Begin to write out your experience.

EXERCISE 5: THE ROUND TABLE

This exercise is intended for those who have practiced active imagination and visualization and feel comfortable working with the exercises in this section. The premise of this exercise is to let those who have inspired you the most over the years solve the creative problem you are facing.

Begin by making list of four people who have inspired you. In a recent class one such list included the musician Dave Mathews, the baroque architect Borromini, the contemporary architect Steven Holl, and the Masai tribe. Set the list aside and begin the exercise.

Loosen any tight-fitting clothing, remove your glasses if you wish, find a comfortable posture, and settle in there. Take a few deep breaths and allow your mind and body to begin to relax. Use a technique such as progressive relaxation or deep breathing and allow yourself to fall into an easy, more serene state where you feel a sense of peacefulness.

Now imagine yourself in a beautiful place in nature, a place you have dreamed about or a favorite place you have visited many times. Take a few moments to experience the peacefulness and the relaxation you find there. Remembering that anything is possible in imagination, invite an inspiring creative advisor to join you at a round table. Allow an image to form that represents that person... accept what comes to you... it may be a wise old man or woman, it may be an animal or a relative or respected teacher. Staying relaxed, ask any question you have concerning your work.

Now listen carefully to the response. It may be a verbal response, it may contain a contain a symbol or image, or it may be something subtle you feel or sense in your body. Just accept what comes to you. If you have another question or are uncertain about the response, feel free to ask another question or invite others who have inspired you to join you at the round table. Now listen to their responses to your question. If any difficulties come to mind with what you are hearing ask for their advice again...What will make things go more smoothly? When you are ready...thank your inspirations for this meeting and ask them how you can best meet again...and when you are ready return to this time and this room, stretch gently, perhaps yawn if you wish, and begin to make notes and prepare to discuss your experience.

As with other active imagination exercises, it is important to ground your experiences by writing them out and discussing them with a trusted friend. You may wish to bring a specific creative problem you are facing or approach the exercise with a more general question. Remember to give yourself time to ground the experience and make sure you will not be interrupted during your work.

Learning to Wrestle

Having activated the inner world, the designer is ready to begin transcribing images and responses. This section describes ways to sustain contact with and deepen our connection to creative states. We want to learn not only how to make an ally of these covert images, but also to develop the capacity to extend their expression into the materialization of the project. Design development really means learning to transcribe your imagination from spirit into matter.

Wrestling with Design Development

There was a time when wrestling was not considered entertainment—it was part of the range of basic life skills. I believe that wrestling trained people to work at close quarters with something or someone that might be unyielding. It taught people the value of having to relate intimately with difficulty and how to fight fairly. To wrestle, you must try to stay on your feet—in other words, in the ego—and not lose hold of what you are trying to pin down. I have always thought of the creative process as a form of wrestling. There is an art to wrestling that requires you to bring a combination of craft, energy, and awareness into the moment.

We cannot avoid obstacles and irreconcilable difficulties when we are trying to create something. Sometimes the point of wrestling is not the victory, but to see if there is a sincere desire to wrestle. In other words, are you willing to fight for your idea? The elders who contemplated the biblical story of Jacob wrestling with the angel have made the point that an angel could easily have wrestled Jacob to the ground—the important question is why the angel allowed Jacob to fight all night. The answer they suggest is that the angel wanted to find out if Jacob was willing to wrestle all night. At dawn, the wrestling ended when the angel withdrew, not wanting to reveal itself. But through the experience of wrestling all night, a bond was created between Jacob and the angel and, as a result, a new name was given to Jacob. His new name was Israel—one who has wrestled all night. Learning how to wrestle means learning how to relate to the divine energies of creation. Everyone who is serious about creating something has trials and stubborn obstacles, so remember that learning through creativity is what will deepen your work and make it more meaningful to yourself and others.

During design development, the designer needs to learn how to wrestle his or her idea down to earth without losing any of its creative power. The primary tool for this transformation is a continuous and evermore precise questioning that is directed toward the first images at the creative heart of the project. This process of testing the idea or inspiration is really a search for the soul of the work. In order for us to find the soul of the work, the work needs to shed its spiritual starting point and acquire physical characteristics.

If wrestling seems to be too dramatic a term to describe the creative experience, then consider for a moment how often the most unexpected kinds of misfortune, mistakes, and illnesses befall designers as they bring their projects to completion. Presenters lose their voices or forget their material. Lack of sleep, psychosomatic illness, and anxiety color our ability to think and create. Students fall off their bicycles and seriously cut themselves before major deadlines. When the unconscious is ignored, it is more than willing to wrestle with our best intentions in order to make itself heard and felt.

Design development ideally brings us to the full integration of drawing, physical modeling, computer-based imaging, and visualization. More and more of the design work can now be accomplished through exposing the project to testing and questioning. The question-and-answer approach is guided by an honest search for the soul of the work. The right question strengthens the work. This ensures that although the project is moving into matter, it is not losing it's spirit. It is becoming stronger and clearer.

The Child in the Adult

As designers, our effectiveness is greatest when we are able to stay in the adult part of the self—the negotiation, follow-through, and

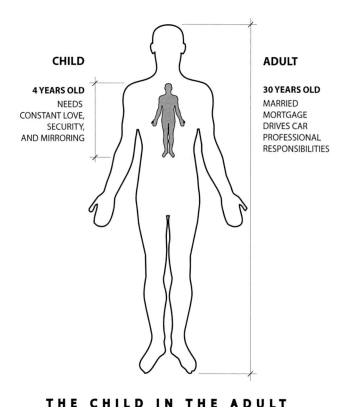

CHILD

4 YEARS OLD
NEEDS
CONSTANT LOVE,
SECURITY,
AND MIRRORING

ADULT

30 YEARS OLD
MARRIED
MORTGAGE
DRIVES CAR
PROFESSIONAL
RESPONSIBILITIES

THE CHILD IN THE ADULT

execution of design decisions need to be in the hands of the adult ego. This seems obvious—none of us would entrust a 6-year-old with making significant decisions about the environment or running an important meeting. Unfortunately, it is not unusual to find that we are unconsciously making decisions and weighing information with the part of ourselves that is not adult. We are "possessed" by the child-like part of ourselves—for a moment, an hour, days, or years—and have allowed that part to steer our decision making. This can be a serious problem. Temper tantrums and the need for constant attention may be acceptable in children, but they are much less satisfying in our colleagues and ourselves. Becoming aware of when we have been possessed by our child-like selves can save us from a great deal of suffering.

The answer is not to suppress, steamroll, or ignore that child-like part of us, but to become aware of our own emotional needs. Once they have been identified, we can take responsibility for our own needs rather than expecting others to mother and father us. There are times when a playful, honest mind is our greatest resource. A raw, stubborn determination may be necessary to safe-guard an important design principle. But there is a great deal of skill required to bring our best decisions through to the built world. The line between child and adult is a fine line that is easily crossed and, once crossed, usually results in endless misdirection, suffering, and confusion. Our work has unconsciously slipped into the part of ourselves that is least equipped to solve the problems we are facing. It is extremely unfair to ask a child to carry responsibil-ity for decision making in areas where he or she has no real expertise or experience. A simple start to addressing this is to work with the above diagram to bring your own adult and childlike needs to the surface and let this knowledge accompany you into the inner studio. This can be done by writing out the childlike and adult qualities you are aware of in yourself. Use this diagram as a way to track this attributes and, if you are experiencing a difficult time, carry it with you.

Drawing First Drawings

Mozart sat down and wrote entire symphonies in a single sitting. Perhaps, for a genius, inspiration comes in such long, sustained pulsations. But for most of us, the act of creation is incremental and involves working with glorious hints and many hard-to-deci-pher moments. It is often a process of three steps forward, followed by at least two steps back. Eight steps forward promises seven steps back. The fortunate thing is that you need very little to begin. All you need are two things: a glimpse, drop, moment, or simple clue, and a willingness to make a drawing that represents that image. That's all you need. If you have that and approach it gently and gather it in and appreciate it, then the act of designing is underway.

There is always a great temptation to get to the end of the proj-ect before a clear beginning has been established. Giving in to this temptation will only make us miss all the important action. How can the act of drawing best accompany imagination on the journey from the mind's eye through to producing an image on a blank sheet of paper?

The word "draw" goes back to the Old English word *dragan*, to drag. The original meaning had to do with coaxing something to appear and causing it to flow out or be forcibly brought out or pulled through a small hole. What are we doing when we draw? On one level, we are making a picture, but we could also be said to be drawing the picture out, either through the mind's eye or through a memory, moment of intuition, or felt experience. Many steps are involved in this process and there may be many pitfalls. We may be wrestling with our expectations or memories of previous projects, or we may be imposing patterns onto this process that are really not part of the present at all. One reason that it is sometimes difficult to show our first images is that, on some level, we are aware that they come from inside us.

"To coax into giving information, to pull together or away, to attract, to evoke..." We have many ways of talking about the project, but what has the greatest affect on the emergence and development of an idea is the state of mind we bring to creativity. The very emotional act and effort of representing the idea can end up repressing it if we ignore our relationship to the inner world. If we are too emotionally driven in our pursuit of a goal, for instance, we may not have the sensitivity to actually receive an image or idea. The awareness that governs relationships on the most sensitive and subtle level of creativity determines whether we are really operating in a receptive way, or whether we are imposing old patterns or opinions on our imagination. During the time of first drawing, we need to remain receptive and not impose any pattern, or have any expectations of a particular outcome. After all, what defines a creative project is that something is being created. We are actually trying to invoke a shift toward being momentarily quiet so that a real insight can arrive.

Fixed points of view, arrogance, and strongly held opinions may be full of energy, but they can all become obstacles to insight and interfere with the process of design imagination. We best serve the creative process by not trying to get something out of it. The moment we feel a strain, we instinctively try to overcome it. We apply more effort and seek to increase the energy being brought to the moment. Another of way of handling this, which is more in accord with your inner world, is to understand the strain as a signal from your inner life, telling you that the present energy, or the present emotional environment, is not conducive to creative work.

This capacity to listen to our energetic signals as a kind of language takes patience and practice. I have been aware of the possibility for many years and still find it much easier to point this out in others than to activate patience within myself. Yet the possibility is there and the results are dramatic when we can practice patience. We can begin by remembering that drawing is the art of recording our discoveries.

When people claim that they have no ideas or that they can't draw, they are usually referring to the other definition of drawing: "to make a picture." At this stage, when the shadow is active, people begin to remember every negative comment they have ever heard about themselves, especially what every careless art teacher or parent commented about their drawing ability. Though these memories and inhibitions can be real, our experience has shown that they don't contribute to creative outcome; they really aren't constructive to the creative work. If you find yourself comparing what you are doing to someone else's work, or if you are putting your own work down, you might make progress by stopping and searching for a more loving attitude to yourself. This is easier said than done, but the important thing is to understand that creativity itself is inherently joyful, and if the creative possibilities are shrinking, compassion is probably undervalued. Sometimes loving yourself is the best way to correct this. This can be as simple as going to meet a friend for coffee.

The other way to minimize the power of negative states is to engage with them. Write them out, or consciously make a time where you agree to allow your "negative designer" a chance to design something for you. This may mean that you take a break at 2 pm and spend 10 minutes letting this part of you express itself.

Let its energy have full expression and love yourself through that process. Then revisit your work afresh.

Drawing as Language

Drawing is a language for transcribing spatial communication, a vehicle for the transportation of an image or spatial idea from a place inside us to the waiting page or computer screen. Hence, the idea of "dragging something out" seems worth examining further. We sometimes feel as though we do have to drag an idea out of ourselves. An image has to be pulled out, pulled along, brought decisively toward us. But the friction doesn't really come from the physical act of drawing–it comes from our internal relationship to creativity.

Drawing has a two-faced character: it is a reflection of the idea and it reflects an internal relationship to the process. In fact, when we draw, we have to be able to do two things at the same time. We have to charm the obstacles while we are focusing our energy on the objective; we have to hold a creative attitude. When these two aspects are balanced, they give the image its energy. Do you feel free to draw? Do you feel free to enjoy the act of drawing? It's like dancing with a pencil, mouse, or paintbrush. Hold your pen, pencil, or mouse as though something precious is coming through the instrument. A dream will often illuminate an unconscious attitude to how we "hold" our creativity. Can you make contact with the joy of expression? If joy is present, we find ourselves free to let images turn and play in the mind's eye. When we can see an image in the mind's eye, even if it is there for only a heartbeat, we have something to draw.

It's the coming into being, the incarnation of this new, balanced energy that we are so moved by when we see it in a drawing or when it makes it all the way into the built thing.

Some Guidelines for Starting Out

1. Design is a contemplative discipline that allows us to learn about our relationship to creativity and about our inner lives. We don't need to know where we are going. In fact, creativity will be sabotaged if we worry too much about where we are going. If it's creative, then the outcome of the journey is veiled.

When the outcome is hidden or unclear, our instinctual and subtle mental perceptions are heightened and that alertness provides us with the sense of being moved that we need to be aware of. We need to get to know the internal phenomena that cause friction, and the useful states of mind that can help bring art into discovery.

2. Images are often first glimpsed–as I have already noted, you only need a glimpse at the beginning. This is important. In the beginning, the design process may happen quickly or slowly. An image that takes seconds to draw is totally adequate and, often, those first briefly glimpsed and recorded images carry surprisingly powerful meanings. They are like an essence and arrive charged with mysterious stories. We are not creating a studied portrait. We only want something to remember the image by. This is necessary because, although we may have written about the image or even described it to others, we may never have seen it. It's like greeting a long-lost friend: you don't know if you will even recognize the person. So we begin by welcoming any aspect of the image, not trying to capture all of it. If we saw the entire thing, it might overwhelm us. Begin with a fleeting glimpse, knowing that it is possible for that glimpse to stand for the entire idea. Our job is to capture, cajole, or trick an image into allowing itself to be transported onto the page. We want to bring nothing into something. The blank page is like a big wide net into which we hope a few lovely birds will fly, birds that we can then set free.

3. The next lesson for drawing out the image comes when we realize that with drawing, we are going to be working with repetition. Since we know that we will not witness the entire concept, we can assume that we will be repeatedly drawing images and that through this iterative process, we are being trained. Repetition is a beautiful part of the development of an idea or image. It introduces us to the ritual of creation and involves us in an ever-deepening search. It introduces us to layering and the complex issue of time, which always begins to appear in the making of something. We have to be in equal measure determined and patient. We are actually clothing the

idea in images that give the project depth and power. A constructed object is going to be saturated by all the thoughts, ideas, images, drawings, and states of mind that went into its creation and fabrication. We are learning to hold this mental space, a space of becoming, while we design. Impossible combinations can come into being and be tested. Skills such as visualization and the intricate, subtle, inner spatial commentary that accompany sophisticated design work are naturally developed and come into play with drawing. Holding a place of becoming in the heart and mind is a basic element of a reflective design practice. It is fundamental to the searching that brings a design through to realization. Designs ripen when imagination, determination, and relaxation can come together.

4. Finally, after the first image has been revealed and worked, we have something. But what exactly is it? It is seldom a direct translation of what we saw in our mind's eye. This is never the time for criticism. We first need to assess what we have. And in order to do this, we often need to work on redrawing the image. This doesn't mean mindlessly copying the image so much as learning to creatively think through the act of drawing. This kind of repetition establishes a cycle whereby verbal questions that probe the intentions, qualities, and ambitions of the project are again and again answered by a drawing. In essence, we are continuing the process of drawing out what is there, but we have now established a dialogue. There is an invisible yet strong line of vibrant communication between the tip of our pens and our image-making faculties. Our thinking is centered in this process. We are pulling out something that already exists in the imagination. The image exists in the mind's eye, perhaps formed of some psychic dust or written in stars across a dark sky inside us. The idea exists on some level of cognition, but does not fully satisfy us until it exists visible and evident on the page. On one level our vocation is to represent and begin to puzzle together what faintly exists. On another level we have to be open to exploring whatever may be obstructing this process.

After producing these first images, it is often very helpful to have other people interpret the drawing because, much like in a dream, these images may have meanings that are so close to us that we can't see them. Or we may be too urgently searching to see what's before us. So it's often helpful to take this new image directly to a friend or trusted colleague and ask him or her to "develop" the image by talking about it or listening as you describe it.

You may wish to experiment with drawing, dragging gently or heavily. There is always more in a drawing than we can see. At this stage, there is no reason to be limited to a drawing. Modeling our heart's desire sometimes brings enormous advantages to the process because we are immediately involved in material and special conditions that set in motion otherwise unseen complexities. A model automatically causes you to consider the plan, section, and perhaps materiality of a project, all at the same time. For some people, working with a model is the most comprehensive and integrating vehicle for the development of a project. Finally, try not to be in a hurry.

The Parti Drawing

At a certain point, we need to make an initial summary of our intentions–this is commonly referred to as a parti drawing. It is not a diagram of the project, but a first embodiment of our heart's desire in the language of design.

Remember that a parti drawing gives organizational intentions to the project. The intention of this drawing is to galvanize preoccupations and perceptions. These drawings and/or models could simply be called representations of "the big idea." A parti drawing expresses organizational qualities, spatial ordering, and, perhaps, something of the proposed character of the project. Depending on your approach to the project, this drawing may be overtly planometric or sectional or generated by an elevation. Any or all of these may form your starting point. Seeing this drawing allows others to understand your "response" to the design problem along a spectrum of possible responses. This drawing is important because it is a generator. It will influence and guide other drawings. We suggest you begin with this drawing in order to focus and test your intentions and ambitions.

To practice this way of seeing the built world, make a parti drawing of the building you are in right now. If you have a favorite place or building, draw it also. This form of drawing conveys a way of seeing that values the spatial organization of things. It is a special kind of coded language that any designer needs to develop in order to communicate the idea-rich language of design. Very few people are skilled across the full spectrum of the design process. More intuitive designers who may be well-versed in "seeing" their creations often struggle when they need to bring these images through into material. Others may find themselves unable to "see" anything, but feel extremely confident when they realize their ideas. The purpose of getting to know your own strengths and weaknesses is that you can consciously bring attention to those places in the design process that will otherwise become stumbling blocks.

Inner and Outer First Critiques

I have not failed. I've just found 10,000 ways that won't work.
–THOMAS EDISON

In my fourth year of studying architecture I hit a roadblock and for an entire term I couldn't design anything. I tried desperately to free myself by working extremely hard for long hours and drinking endless cups of thick coffee, but nothing seemed to help. I hated to admit it, but I was stuck and felt completely humiliated. It was a confusing and depressing experience that I had seen strike others but never thought that I would fall victim to. In the end, I managed to scrape through with a project I didn't like and can no longer remember.

Looking back, I know that the problem wasn't the difficulty of the assignment, but the fact that I had encountered the great enemy of design–a self-critical attitude and extreme judgment. My intense struggle to improve the design had somehow made it worse and taken away any chance of improving the project. It's worth mentioning this right away because criticism and judgment are valuable and necessary tools during the development of a project, yet they have the power to completely inhibit creativity. While design is best nourished by generous helpings of freedom and imagination, what is the right role of criticism?

First we need to look at the difference between inner and outer critics. The inner critic is the way we talk to ourselves, using phrases like "I'm no good...I can't do this...I have nothing to say...my ideas are never worth saying...." These are words that we may have learned from critical teachers or parents when we were growing up. The judgments and negativity expressed will stop us in our tracks. The reason they continue to have power over us is that we still believe that these comments are true. They remind us of what it was like to hear these comments as children, and the vivid sense of hurt or anger or sadness that we felt then is activated and overwhelms any creative impulse. Obviously, when we are caught in the child and we experience inner judgment and negativity, we will not be able to make wise decisions.

The way to free ourselves from the negative power of judgment is to become conscious of the comments, perhaps write them out and see if we can find their source. Where did we hear these words? Who said them to us? The very act of writing them out and analyzing them puts us in the position of being the adult. It is the adult part of us that is capable of seeing through these opinions and discovering what is true. The outer critic will use the same messages and, though we are free to respond, it is usually much too difficult because the comments trigger hurtful memories from long ago. Rather than being destructive, criticism should serve the development of design through constructive comments that do not undermine the designer. The questioning, evaluating, discussing, and analyzing should help the latent qualities of the design emerge and bring out the highest and best aspirations of the project. Constructive criticism moves the design toward a more organized, advanced, refined, and clear state so that it can become more useful to its future users and more satisfying to its designer.

Criticism becomes a destructive experience when an unconscious desire for perfection or power overwhelms the conscious attitude. The desire for perfection can send a wave of critical comments that will easily undo a project, particularly one that belongs to an inexperienced designer. The use of criticism for power, in order to go "one up" on the designer, whether out of a sense of competition or a need to be superior, is always damaging to creative work.

This is extremely important because if we were to measure the time spent creating and designing and developing a project, we would probably find as much time is spent internally or externally assessing the project as is spent drawing it. Everything in the built world rests on lengthy periods of discussion and the tenor of these discussions can easily find its way into the project. Multiply the influence of these unconscious states of design on the number of projects being created and you begin to understand why our world looks, works, and feels the way it does.

Generating Creative Inventory

If a project is criticized and judged too often or too early in the creative cycle of development, it simply will not be able to thrive and grow. But if a project goes too long without any review, it may not be worth completing. For this reason, the timing of criticism is crucial in the production of good design.

Design development assumes that criticism is applied to the work by degrees, so that the criticism always fits the stage of design throughout the development cycle of the work. The energy required to create is often fragile, and this sensitivity won't withstand premature criticism. For this reason, it's useful to establish a judgment-free zone at the start of the project. The psyche needs to feel free to let ideas churn and reverberate. The slowing down of an idea needs to take place when it encounters complexity, not self-doubt. Let the material you encounter as your project develops do that work for you! This doesn't mean that anything that is created is appropriate and must be venerated, but experience indicates that society suffers less from buildings that collapse than from wonderful creative ideas that are squashed and defeated. I see this caused by a negative collective unconscious belief that has its root in an overly critical attitude that is fearful of creativity and pleasure.

First Stage: Preliminary Design

It makes the most sense to invite a critique of a project after the creative direction and basic design language have been established. The question that needs to be answered is, "Does the proposition stand up to local or global review? Is there a convincing demonstration of the benefits of the proposition?" Is the big idea capable of carrying the project into the world?

If you are prone to severe self-criticism and impatience, then you may find you are unable to internally grow an idea to its richest outcome. You may need to get to know your critical voice and consciously recognize it when it possesses you so that you can shift to the part of you that believes the project is worthwhile and worthy of being successfully completed. This doesn't mean that you should allow your ideas to go untested. But initial testing must always have the intention not of attacking the work, but helping to search for the truth of the founding idea in the project. If a critique is constructive, it addresses the substance of the idea. As the idea becomes more and more substantial, the proposition will naturally need more rigorous testing.

Designers are always searching for certainty, something that, in the cycle of design, is constantly shifting. Our bodies, dreams, and shadow are always available to us to deepen our sense of knowing the true course of our work. The reason that we need to bring an awareness of these phases to the creative process is that there is a real danger of activating critical states that will destroy creative impulses. And, as we have seen, the compounded result of these acts is that, eventually, the artifacts and places of the built world transmit these negative messages. For the designer, once the creative impulse is muted or deadened, it may be very difficult to bring its rich voice back to our task.

PART FIVE

Using This Life to Be Creative and Wise

The purpose of life is to be defeated by greater and greater things.
–Rainer Maria Rilke

A local inventor devoted himself to designing a machine that would grow lettuce in half the time it takes to grow in a field. He had rented a factory and his prototype sat like a robotic lunar module in the center of the big industrial space. The seeds went in one end and his goal was to have perfect lettuce come out the other end. He reasoned that since plants only need nutrients and sunlight to grow, his machine would completely optimize these conditions by eliminating the time a plant spent in the darkness of night, thus allowing the lettuce to grow to maturity in half the time nature needed. The problem he constantly ran into was that, although only modest growth took place at night, the enormous amount of chemical activity that occurred within the plant in the dark was crucial to all of its development. He continues to work on his machine, but he can't find a way to replace the time of darkness where "nothing" seems to happen.

The Four Functions

Why are there so many ways to be in a state of muddleness, but only very few ways to be tidy?
–Gregory Bateson

"Form follows function" has probably become the world's best-known modern design strategy. Broadly interpreted, it suggests that a thing, whether it is at the scale of a building or a kitchen appliance, is in some essential way like skin draped over action; it is designed from its function outward. This complex and elegant thought has been a central idea of modernism since it was first uttered by Louis Sullivan more than 100 years ago. Around the same time, Carl Jung presented a way of understanding personalities called the Four Functions. His proposal went on to form the basis of the Myers Briggs Test. Jung's approach offers a psychological approach to function that explores how we innately approach life's challenges. One proposition sees form residing in the function of the building; the other would see design residing in the way the personality functions. No two individuals will approach a problem the same way. Everyone has their own way to be creative and to understand things. The purpose of the Four Functions is to help you get to know your own best way to approach things.

About a third of the way into a design project, two students were stuck. Jason had no difficulty in organizing all the elements of the project in a reasonable way. He had thought about the parts of the building and had arranged everything logically. The building functioned well enough, but he really couldn't say very much about the life of the building. The plan of the building had become a diagram. He knew the best place to locate most things, but not how the daily rituals of living would breathe life into the place and give it its special character. The human side of the design was a mystery to him.

Jean had developed a much less obvious plan, but she was overflowing with feelings about the project and enthusiastically imagined all kinds of wonderful settings for social intercourse throughout the building. It became obvious, however, that none of these were going to be realized because she couldn't bring any thinking to help her structure all the wonderful ideas she had.

Both Jason and Jean were stuck: they knew their projects lacked something, but they didn't know how to incorporate or activate the missing component. Jean's project embodied what was missing from Jason's project. Jason had all the clarity that was missing from Jean's project. In both cases the designs were suffering an imbalance. Although Jason was a strong thinker, his feeling about the life of the building had not been activated. Jean's work was dominated by her feelings, but her thinking had not found a way to order the project. As you might expect, Jean's drawings were dense with layers of graphite, while Jason's images were clear computer-generated sheets.

Both of the above kinds of buildings get built. The built world puts us in direct contact with what is unconscious in the designer. Neither student could shift his or her approach to include the psychological function that was missing from the design. The part of the designer that was least conscious was least developed, and it was therefore unavailable when needed to complete the design. In order to understand this idea we need to explore the Four Functions.

Jung's four primary functions–thinking, feeling, sensing, and intuition–were arranged to form a quaternary. He believed that each person relies on a primary function, a vehicle for the personality that is innately developed in us and that we naturally use to accomplish tasks and navigate the world. The hallmark of the primary function is that we feel at home with it when we use it. Two of the other functions are supportive though less developed, and one function is considered inferior and is not usually consciously developed. When the inferior function is required, we feel very uncomfortable because we are being asked to use something we don't know much about. In fact, when we see another person whose strength is a function we consider to be "inferior," we actually may not like them and think they are stupid or confused! In our example, how could Jason bring more feeling to his design work if he wasn't aware that feelings might have something to offer the design process? Besides, his thinking was very developed and had "solved" the problem. On the other hand, Jean would not trust her thinking to solve something because she didn't believe it was necessary to bring "thinking" to creative work. Obviously her strong feeling function had always powered her work.

For most of us, it is only through getting stuck that we have any reason to enter into a dialogue with the part of ourselves that is less developed. And this is precisely the deeper value that obstacles and challenges have for us during the design experience. Feelers believe that thinking is crude and less sophisticated than feeling, just as thinkers tend to believe that feelings are crude and unhelpful intruders in the design process. Becoming aware of these internal opposites is important because they often present us with an opportunity to bring "what is missing" to our project. The unwanted and unfamiliar aspect, the so-called inferior function, is often the very "trouble" we need to incorporate to grow or free our work.

Jung suggested that around the mid-point of life, the function that had been inferior would need to be consciously developed in order to contribute to and refresh the task of growing into a fully integrated human being. What I have noticed is that this mid-point is no longer around the age of 40; it may be experienced much earlier if we are interested in becoming more conscious. I have found this concept to be a useful guide in actualizing design understanding and working through design process.

One student, when asked what was driving his project, insisted that he wanted the building to be made of stone. He kept repeating that the building needed to be thick; as he talked you could feel his richly developed "sense" of the project. He was sure of this one point, but, as a sensing type, he was missing the intuitive capacity to see the big picture. An intuitive, on the other hand, begins with a proposal that usually incorporates an overview, a global understanding of the enterprise. Intuitive types often lose interest in a project after they "see" the project in their mind's eye. They see no reason to complete the project because they already see it completed! Thinking types believe in a rational basis for making design decisions. For example, the spaces of the house will be rationally configured, which is positive, but what happens when it is time to discuss the social life of the house? Will a rational approach create hiding places or places to play? A feeling type might be totally centered on the emotional quality the house transmits, but may be unable to organize a design that can contain these qualities. A designer whose main function revolves around sensing will have a strong "sense" of the materials they wish to use before anything else has come into focus, and they may be most comfortable building a model of what they are trying to create.

The purpose of identifying our dominant functions is that it helps us to understand our strengths and weaknesses during the creative process. It's a self-diagnosing design tool to use when you get stuck and it supports a full-bodied approach to design of the built world. If design does not have a desire to integrate all of our psychic anatomy, how will we ever feel at home in the built world? When it comes to the process of design, form does follow function- the dominant function. Getting stuck may be the result of wearing out a particular function, a moment when a new point of view is needed. The overvaluation of rational thinking may be remedied by asking questions about the feeling of the place. Similarly, too much intuition may need the grounding influence of the sensing function with its love of craft and materiality.

No one function is superior to another. Our most interesting experiment may be to consciously involve as full an array of functions as possible in the project. Over time, we may notice that the places and ways we get stuck repeat themselves. The experience is familiar to us, not only because we have noticed it before, but also because we have seen the very sequence of events that led to getting stuck many times before. At the very least, we can approach a project as a chance to learn about ourselves and see the project from four different perspectives. After all, building users will come from every category, as will clients, contractors, and civic officials. Our goal is to be able to access and enjoy all four functions.

Working with Your Strengths and Weaknesses

Some people love to draw. Others are really good at talking about their work. Some can describe the most wonderful things to you, but they find it impossible to draw anything. Some love to make models and others just like to stew on things and not start until the creative pressure builds up inside them. Each of these approaches describes a way of creating that links back to a function. Everyone has his or her own way of creating. A general approach is to begin with several streams of work. Draw it, speak it, and write it–this way you are less likely to get stuck. Always have a fresh relationship to your ideas. The stewing time is what you do when you move between the three modes.

Jung suggested that when we become identified with our principle function, we look down on our inferior function. The problem is that we then begin to look down on other people who may have this as their principle function. From this observation, we can understand the value of not becoming too identified with out own principle function and the value of self-reflection, particularly when your relational world becomes charged.

Thinking Too Much

It is not uncommon in the design process to find ourselves "overthinking" what we are doing and blocking our own creativity. But like the other ways of getting stuck, thinking too much has a role to play in design.

How do we recognize when we are thinking too much? The first step is to become aware and accept that it is happening, so that we can make a conscious decision to do something about it. The next step is to find out exactly what is going on. Becoming conscious, aware, or mindful of what we are actually doing is like turning on a light. Once we have shed some light on the situation, we can see what is happening and know what to do. Awareness gives us access to more of our resources and helps us make better decisions. It is also a gift because it allows us learn about the parts of ourselves that we may have lost or given away long ago.

Obsessing about something or someone is not the same as thinking too much. If that is what we are doing, we need to find out why we are projecting so much of our mental energy onto that person or thing. Why are we not putting this energy into ourselves? If we're obsessing about whether we will be successful or not, then we need to ask why it is so important to us? We may never have realized that we are putting so much life energy into this. We may not even know what we want or what moves us. We may never have asked the question, "What are my personal needs and desires?"

If our obsessive thinking is about our need to control people and events around us, we need to become aware of it. If we accept our need to control, if we acknowledge that we are capable of acting this way, then it becomes easy to decide what we would like to do about it. Sometimes the issue is that our ego is not strong and we don't have the strength to control our own emotions, so we become controlling and critical of others. Why do we need to sometimes control our environment as though it is a life or death issue? Why is every situation so stressful? When we are willing to investigate our shadow we will stop projecting it onto others. The energy that has gone into projecting our shadow can now begin to strengthen ourselves and allow our creativity to emerge.

Similarly, if we are genuinely not able to relate to other people because we live too much in our own heads, then we need to become aware of it. How does it make us feel? Is this what we want? How did we become so cut off from our feelings? What caused us to decide that feelings are not a legitimate source of truth? Again, if we become aware, we can make a decision to do something about it. We may decide that is time to learn what it would be like to be living in our bodies. As we do this, we may run up against our judgments about our bodies or feelings. We may experience how difficult it is for us to trust anything or anyone. We may only know how to trust our thoughts! We may never have felt any compassion for our bodies though all the years that they have served us faithfully. We may never have bothered to relate with our bodies' symptoms and desires. We may be complete strangers to our own feelings. We can use an awareness of living in our heads to lead us to a richer experience of what it means to be a human being.

Getting Stuck

Getting stuck is the darkness that is inevitable and even necessary to every inspiring journey.

How is it that something we worry about and fear can actually help us? Because you can use everything–every experience, every circumstance, everything around you–to learn something about yourself and your creative instincts. As I discussed earlier, Carl Jung argued that whatever we ignore will happen to us as fate. We experience difficulties because the psyche wants us to learn some-thing from them and, at the same time, the difficulties would not arise unless we had the means to learn from them. Every time we turn away from these experiences, every time we ignore difficulty, we can be assured that it will reappear in some form in the near future. This is a law of the psyche: it wants us to be whole and healthy and find that balanced tension that is so essential to creativity. Difficulty, setbacks, and failure can never be eliminated. But we can lose our ability to learn from them.

Getting stuck is a natural and necessary part of the creative process, a crucial moment in the design journey. Of course, every-one would like to design great projects and never get stuck, but in truth, every designer goes through phases of feeling blocked. Getting stuck always presents us with an opportunity to deepen our projects. It is a message from within our own depths that we need to make a change in our direction. Physical symptoms can tell us this, so can dreams, and so can the shadowy world of the creative process itself.

The creative process is filled with mistakes and trials, not because we lack skills, but because we grow through difficulty. Getting stuck is the inbuilt mechanism for growth in the creative process, for getting input from the unconscious. Getting stuck can manifest in any number of ways—frustration, headaches, self-doubt, anger, and boredom are just some of the ones I have experienced. These roadblocks, dead-ends, and soul-searching detours are the unpredictable happenings that deepen, enhance, and make real the work of a designer. Because difficulties are inevitable, it makes sense to use the conflict creatively when it comes, rather than using our energy to avoid it or hope it will not come. We are trying to bring our heart's desire into matter and it's natural that there is almost a chemical reaction as these two worlds are brought together.

Getting stuck is an unconscious message that we have missed the chance to incorporate some important aspect of the project. It is often the shadow aspect of a project that brings us the very essence of what needs to be incorporated. We have been called to step back and examine our work from a new point of view, and with this new perspective, we may learn something that will support what great projects are made of. The most important thing to accept is the most difficult to accept: getting stuck is a natural part of the creative journey. The first task is to see if you can accept getting blocked without taking it personally and losing the creative dimension of the project. It takes courage to surrender and avoid action. Creative journeying is just like other kinds of travel–it's filled with moments of no movement. These periods when projects come to a standstill, are as important as times when projects move forward. You don't want to miss them. Standing still can be a very intense but exciting stage of the work. Over time it will become apparent that when we get stuck, empathy has more to offer than aggression. If you ignore the messages of getting stuck and force the project to completion, it will be dispirited. If you accept and don't force the creative impulse, it will naturally reassemble, redirect, recharge, and refocus itself, and present itself again in the form of a new idea, a new impulse, a new direction.

In the same way that faith cannot be forced, creativity and imagination will not respond to being forced. The ego cannot create inspiration, but it can help with our determination and resolve. When you don't know what to do, don't do anything. Surrender. Think of "getting stuck" as a benevolent guest who has arrived to give you a message. If you treat this guest well, your project will go through a new cycle of growth that will benefit you and the world. There is a well-known story in architectural circles about Louis Kahn asking a brick what it wanted to be. Why not ask your project why it is stuck? You may hear the intelligence inherent in a creative work telling you what is missing. Students often know when they have avoided an important piece of information or intuition that is needed to complete a project. Listening to "getting stuck" is a difficult discipline. No one wants to be patient; these things are learned through difficult trials. A creative work is a living thing and does not like being bossed around or dictated to. These approaches are recipes for taking the soul out of your work–you may get it finished, but it won't make anyone happy.

When you are making no progress, you may feel destroyed, but the creative process isn't destroyed, it's totally intact. The process is clearly telling you that movement right now is not wise. This is usually the moment when we start to feel afraid of failing–"I'm doomed" "This project is doomed" "I shouldn't be an architect".... The despair isn't helpful because judgment is the opposite of creation. Everything gets worse because imagination cannot function when judgment is present and we lose the relaxation that is so necessary for creative work. If you find yourself caught in a negative vortex, take a deep breath and go out for a brisk walk.

Creativity is more cyclic than linear. The process may seem to move along a linear path in later production stages, but the first wave of creative process is more about wandering, getting lost, getting found, stumbling through things, trying elusive flavors, and experimenting with new tastes. Imagination and the unconscious come with their own ideas about space and time. If you ignore them, they won't cooperate and you will cut your work off from their remarkable creative capacities. They are seeking a space in which to manifest, and your relaxed awareness and relationship to the process can create that space. This simply means we need to remember that special laws of space and time operate in the creative world and we need to tune into them.

Another reason that aggression or willfulness is not effective when you are trying to be creative is that energy that is busy pursuing and pushing hasn't the sensitivity to receive. Creative impulses need a chance to make an impression on the conscious mind. When we feel stuck, we are being asked to wait patiently while the psyche sorts through impressions or silently wrestles with unseen dimensions of the problem.

The experience of "letting go" is often the quickest way of learning from obstacles and difficulties. Letting go is not the same as giving up. Letting go means not resisting. Not resisting means staying connected to how you are feeling in the present moment. When you resist, you are cut off from your creative instincts. Letting go connects us with the present moment and this kind of attention always brings creativity and wisdom. Giving up has the feel of resignation, of being unable to move forward, of being the victim of circumstance. Letting go is not like this. Letting go is surrendering consciously.

When you get stuck, be sure to consciously stop for a moment. Really stop as fully as possible. Our creative pause is akin to the way we react to a stop sign when we are driving. We slow down, we begin to stop, but at the last moment we decide to keep moving. The stopping I am describing is like turning off the motor, getting out of the car, and taking a deep breath. Let go of trying to resolve anything. Let go, set free, and do not judge is the mantra to recall when difficulty strikes. As Jung once said, "In the hour of reconciliation, great marvels appear."

12 Ways of Getting Stuck

We must be able to let things happen in the psyche.
–C.G. JUNG

With any form of getting stuck, if you look at the block realistically you will come to see that it is valuable and it has a purpose. This step is very important because if you accept that every block has an origin, you are on your way to transforming it. Your creative drive is capable and agile and wants to learn from obstacles, so why not make good use of whatever is obstructing your path.

1. "I'm spinning my wheels"

If you feel as though you are spinning your wheels, the message may be that you don't need to be pressing on the gas pedal at all. Stop making an effort to create. Spinning your wheels may indicate that you have lost creative traction with the project and your current point of view is out of touch. Take your foot off the gas. Let yourself come to a complete stop. Let your emotions come to a stop. Stop trying! When did you last feel that you had a good grip on the work? When you are stuck, you sometimes need to back up to go forward. You may already have everything you need to go forward and your pressing for additional material is the problem. You may be ignoring the idea you already have that can carry you to completion. Go back to those drawings, ideas and notes and see if there is really a need for "more." All that you may need to do is carefully develop what you have, rather than trying to bring new material to the project. The sensation of spinning your wheels may simply be telling you that you are trying too hard.

2. "I'm bored"

Marion was working on the design of a Chinese cultural center. She sat at her desk looking annoyed and upset. She had a site and had done good preliminary work, but found herself stuck. Finally she said, "I'm really bored with this project. I don't want to do a cultural center." She sounded frustrated. She had been very enthusiastic a few weeks ago and now she found herself totally bored and worried the project was dead, that "it is all wrong," that she would have to start again. It was like a promising relationship that now seemed unworkable. After a little silence I said, "Let's see what we can learn from boredom." Marion began to say she wanted to stop working in the way she had planned. Then she related how she had heard another student complain about how terrible a new Chinese cultural center she had visited had been. And suddenly Marion said she really felt drawn to design a daycare center and a theater along with some special housing. Suddenly it became clear that this new vision was the cultural center! The old idea of a cultural center had been boring–she couldn't even work on it. And listening to the boredom–trusting the boredom and letting the energy of boredom and frustration express itself–allowed for the release of a new creative pulsation. The cultural center went from being a static, curated institution to a vibrant cauldron of unpredictable interactions and the culture of the project was born. As is so often the case, the layer underneath the first message was rich and alive, waiting to emerge from its chrysalis.

It's important to listen to boredom. Becoming aware of feeling bored is the beginning of reconnecting to your creative instincts. Boredom is a clear signal telling you to stop. Don't go further along the path until you can do so without boredom. Chances are your work is about to take an unexpected turn. Perhaps a sacrifice is necessary. What aspect of the project might you have to sacrifice to go further? What image do you have of yourself as designer that may need to be surrendered to move forward?

3. "I've got too many ideas"

Sometimes during a project you are faced with a situation in which you have several promising ideas that pull you in different directions. All of them seem worthwhile for very different reasons and you find yourself caught up in inner dialogues, attempting to convince yourself of first one and then another possibility, but without any clear sense of which is right. The answer may come from beginning to do all three. Why negate any possible options at this stage? The key is to work with all of the creative energy. Carry all of the possibilities into the creative heat of the work. Give up knowing exactly what to do and trust the positive material. It's never a good idea to turn away from creative material. Rather than debating with your work, let go and let your heart's desire enjoy all the ideas you have. Any additional stress caused by this approach will help heighten your personal sense of desire for what you like. There is no need to abandon any of your creative instincts. Everything can be brought forward. A useful rule of thumb for projects that feel stuck or when momentum is fragile is to go with the positive emotion and let that energy liberate you from the obstacles.

Karen had only few days left to complete an assignment and she didn't know what to do. She had several good ideas, each leading in a different direction, and she didn't know which to pursue. "Should I do this one or go with that one?" she asked. I looked over her work it and agreed that she had several good ideas. Finally I said, "Why not do all of them. Just keep going with all three." She just looked at me and I could tell that she was thinking, *Are you crazy! I have only six days left! That's a stupid suggestion. I don't have the time to do all of them.* So I said to her, "You probably think I'm crazy to suggest that you do all of them because you don't have time to do all them. Which one do you want to do?" And she started to laugh and somehow gathered up the resolve to make the decision that had been holding her back. There is nothing wrong with acknowledging that time is a factor in what can be accomplished. The deadline is helpful in that it creates the finite container for our work. Accept that perfection is not only impossible, but it also brings an attitude that blocks any chance of enjoying the creative process.

4. "I don't think I can do this"

Stop what you are doing. You may need to free yourself from self-judgment, a common form the negative shadow can take. When you are too hard on yourself you can easily lose your bearings. A quick way to identify this is to simply write down what you are thinking about yourself. The antidote to negative thoughts is not to debate with them, but to become conscious of them and release yourself from believing them. You may need to do something you used to really like to do, no matter how simple, absurd, or strange. If you have completely lost your confidence, you will probably need to spend time with your heart's desire before returning to the project. If you have a friend who you trust to listen to this aspect of your work, have him or her take notes while you describe the essence and passion of what you want to do. If your lack of confidence persists, try writing out the negative statement you are saying to yourself. Putting it on paper will distance you from its grip. Remember your gut will tell you what to do and your head will tell you how. What do you want? Use your ability to think positively in order to strategize a path towards your goal.

5. "They said my project is terrible"

Did the criticism you received about your project remind you of something you've heard before? Was it like the voice of someone you know? Did the critical words trigger a particular phrase you heard years ago? You may have been remembering and getting stuck in the feeling of what it was like to be criticized by a parent or teacher when you were a child. Chances are that assigning the critical voice to its source will loosen its grip and its negative power will decline. Most difficult to spot are those times when we are the source of our own negative voice. We may have a tendency to unconsciously criticize our own work in a way that affirms a destructive and negative belief. Are you doing what you love to do? If the answer is yes, then stay true to what you love and ask a friend for an independent assessment of your work. If you consistently think negatively about your work, talk to a counselor.

However, if after reflection you are convinced that your project is not terrible, if your gut tells you that what you have done is right and clearly energizing, then you have no choice but to keep on going. The courage to go your own way even if it means breaking a rule cannot be taught. Fighting for your ideas and refusing to be stopped by what other people think can mark the beginning of becoming an adult.

6. "I'm always getting stuck near the end of the project"

There may be a shadow aspect that needs to be made conscious. We may believe at an unconscious level that we do not have the right to be successful. We may be living under the spell of old programming that has "possessed" us. Do you really believe that you have the right to successfully finish a project. Do you really believe that you have the right to be happy?

Take a deep breath and fill your lungs with air. Let your shoulders relax and let your jaw soften. Let your skin soften. Close your eyes and see if you can imagine yourself in your mind's eye as a designer. What image comes to you? Draw yourself as a designer. Where are you? How do you look? Perhaps a part of you feels sore or stiff. Imagine that part of you as a designer. Draw your body at the computer or drawing table. Who is standing around you?

7. "It doesn't matter what I do—I feel like giving up"

When you're feeling hopeless or despairing about your project you may want to imagine how others may benefit from it. How could your work be helpful to the world. Dedicate the project to the welfare of others and vow to design a project that gives good conditions to the world. Or think of someone who has helped you in your life and inwardly dedicate the project to him or her. Complete the project in a way that honors those who have helped you. It is easy to get self-absorbed when undertaking a creative project. Asking yourself how the project is helpful to others can expand the boundaries of a design.

Another approach involves designing as a ritual in which you purposely design a really hopeless place. Try expressing yourself through a design exercise as a way of becoming conscious of the emotion. Take a good look at what you create and then throw it away!

8. "I've got a headache"

Put your pen or pencil down, take your hand off the mouse, allow yourself to let go. Close your eyes, take a deep breath, and as you exhale let your shoulders drop and your face soften. After a few normal breaths, direct a question inward to your headache or to the tension in your body. Ask the suffering part of yourself to comment on the best way toward a healthy resolution, saying, for instance, "Dear headache, I am ready to listen to you...what do you need from me?" You may be surprised by the earthy, grounded advice you receive.

You may need to take a walk or breathe fresh air. You may need to sleep. You may need to stop thinking. You can write to your headache or perhaps write a letter as though your headache wishes to communicate with you. The discomfort of a headache is a form of communication that needs to be listened to if it is to transform into a more useful type of energy. We want to learn to hear its message and then understand where it is coming from. Remember that whatever your headache has to say is only the first part of the exercise. The exercise is completed when you can bring its answer into your project. For example, when you are trying too hard, you may literally be gripping your pen too tightly or straining through your hand, arm, and shoulder. You may be holding your head in a way that stresses your entire body. All of these conditions are going to find their way consciously or unconsciously into your work and are likewise experiences that can be transformed into new ways your project can release, expand, or soften in its realization.

9. "I feel as though I'm on a roller coaster of hope and despair"

The creative process can offer great highs and great lows. Sometimes these moods are completely intertwined. Sometimes demons have the upper hand, and sometimes the muses are victorious. Over time you will get to know more and more of the feeling of both aspects of yourself. The best place to be in the creative process is the middle, but the very identification with design that makes it so much fun also brings these emotions. Try to remain in contact with your inner voice and its knowing way of directing design sensibilities. With experience, we can stay in the middle of greater and greater turmoil rather then trying so hard to eliminate it. It can be helpful to imagine what you think your favorite designer or a respected elder would do when faced with your difficulty. What advice have they for you? Let them bring you back to your center.

There is another benefit in this often difficult and perplexing situation: your project acquires its genuine and authentic character from surviving these journeys. No abstraction or intellectualization obscures the true nature of the project. Your sorrow or your excitement, if you can stay connected to them, will ultimately enrich your project. Through this process, what you design—and who you are—will be strengthened. This experience brings an element of earthbound inspiration to your work.

Sometimes it can useful to just play. What brought you joy when you were younger, before you thought of becoming a designer? What ignited your enthusiasm? Whatever that activity was, try returning to it and just play. If you like to dance, play soccer, or play a musical instrument, bring this into your daily routine.

10. "I can't let go of an idea—but it's not working"

Frank was designing a university building for a small town, and from the very first sketches had insisted on there being a large tower rising out of the center of the building. Repeated reviews and critiques from teachers had questioned his strategy and finally dismissed the tower as a "bad idea." What was interesting was that Frank would not or could not let go. After six weeks of intense and heated debate, his tower had grown slightly smaller, but its appeal was a mystery to everyone. Frank was really stuck and increasingly worried. He could not go forward or backward. What helped him was a simple question, repeated several times, that he was asked to carefully reflect on: "Frank, ask yourself—why is this tower so important to you?" He needed to enter into an active imagination exercise with the tower. When I teach, my position is always to see where the design will go. How will the project unfold and evolve and how will the designer go through this process? Frank was stuck on the tower and this was blocking every creative impulse. What had first inspired him had somehow drained the project of any creative juices. It was a mistake.

Finally some creative sparks began to rise and the role of the tower began to drop right into its large public base. The project began to transform as the energy and desire that had been invested in one gesture started to infuse the entire project. A whirlwind of creative ideas broke through and the building started to come alive. In the end, you might say the tower had been necessary–it had a role to play in the design process–but not the role Frank had at first imagined. It showed Frank the implications of bringing a rigid approach to the act of design. It also showed him what a mistake felt like (it felt draining and depressing), and most importantly that he could survive his mistakes. He didn't have to be afraid of letting them go. It is really helpful to know that you can learn from a mistake. Mistakes are among our most valuable teachers and will help move our design work forward if we can learn from them. The creative process loves paradox and so it is not unusual to find that you have to let go of what you have to get what you want.

11. "I don't have anything"/ "Nothing I try seems to work"

I was sitting around a table with four students. It was a design seminar at the start of a large project. The students had been working on the assignment for two days. Each student was asked to show their work and then participate in a group discussion of their project. The first student, Marie, began by opening her sketchbook to a page that had three pencil drawings. The first was an idea for the spatial organization of the building. The second sketch was an idea for the vertical relationships showing a section through the building, and the final drawing was an interior sketch perspective of the major public space. She began by saying she didn't have very much to show, and then she talked about her proposal for 10 minutes, taking us through all of her ideas in considerable detail. She completed her presentation by apologizing for not having very much. She sounded indifferent and spoke without much confidence.

When she finished, I asked the other three students at the table, "If you worked for Marie, and she gave you this presentation, could you produce a comprehensive design for the building?" Everyone nodded enthusiastically. Everyone felt inspired by her proposal. It is equally possible to look at a page of drawings and see only scraps of raw ideas or, alternatively, you might see all that you need to design a large complex building. "I don't have very much" isn't always about the project. Sometimes it's about a lack of confidence or encouragement. It's interesting that others may be satisfied and enthusiastic about a design while its author may feel snagged by a lack of confidence.

There can be an experience during the creative process in which all paths seem futile. There is little or no joy in the work and the fear that the entire enterprise will collapse takes hold. This leads to an overwhelming feeling of doom and gloom and it really seems as though there is no chance of salvaging the work–there is a complete lack of hope. In this case, it may be worth trying to use the negative mood to energize the ego. This involves bringing the negative point of view to life through design. If you were designing a garden, then try to design a garden for someone exactly like your-self, someone who is afflicted with a dark mood. What kind of place would be welcoming or would express your state of being? If you were designing a house, imagine that the client is "down." What kind of house would match their mood? This externalizing of an emotion may generate an idea or release a block that will liber-ate the weight of the difficulty. Often the most direct way to free yourself of a block is to give the problem you are facing to someone else. Using the active imagination technique, simply imagine inwardly what your favorite designer, poet, or filmmaker would do, and bring their experience and wisdom to consciousness.

12. "I can't stand the people I'm working with"

Jung felt that the characteristics that bother us most in others derive their power from the fact that they show us something inside ourselves that we think is unacceptable. If I am bothered by some-one's selfishness, I may need to develop my capacity to nurture myself. If it upsets me that my colleague jumps to conclusions, then I may need to do a better job of honoring my own intuitive-ness. In choosing to not blame the other, I choose instead to try growing in places within myself that I may have difficulty acknowl-edging. The key to managing interpersonal situations is to own the shadow side of ourselves. The hallmark of the shadow is often its exaggerated response. A phrase or a glance that makes us wild with a theory of conspiracy or attack is a sign that we may be possessed by our shadow. It is very difficult to acknowledge one's own shadow. One technique is to try writing a description of yourself that acknowledges the behavior you find upsetting as something you are capable of from time to time. If this fails to help, try visu-alizing your enemy happy. See them smiling in nature. If this is not possible, try to see yourself in light and happy; once you can do this, try again with your enemy. If this is not possible try to visual-ize something you care about, like a plant or pet or perhaps your room. Once you find something you can send affection toward, try to work your way back to sending the affection to yourself and then perhaps your enemy.

When you get stuck, the most important thing is to believe in your own creativity. To do this you need to consciously have the experi-ence of being creative. Because everyone is creative, you may never have actually stopped to ask yourself what it feels like when you are creative. You need to give yourself permission to know and enjoy the experience in your body and mind when you are moved and possessed by the creative spirit. This is a fundamental part of every-one and can easily be obscured by the pressures to succeed and be liked. What we sometimes forget is that this part of ourselves is indestructible and always available.

Go back in your mind to a creative moment you enjoyed and try to recall the sensation in your body and mind. See if you can reconstruct and really enjoy the sensation of the creative moment physically moving through you. If you have trouble making contact with a feeling of being creative, ask yourself what moves you. You may need to go to an art gallery and find a painting or sculpture you like. Rather then analyzing the experience, just allow yourself to stand in front of the work of art. Rest in the feeling of being moved by a favorite object. You may need to dance to a favorite song or walk through a vibrant part of your city. Once you have made contact with what moves you, try closing your eyes and see if you can make contact with the feeling of the creative impulse in your body. Open your eyes and revisit the source of your inspiration. I often suggest to designers who are in a funk about their talent that they go to a store that sells things they love. It may be cars or shoes, furniture or electronics—the point is not to make a purchase but to make direct contact with your desires.

What I have noticed most often is that designers don't anchor themselves deeply enough in the enjoyable feeling of what inspires them. There is lots of analysis of these places and artifacts, but the feelings about them are not valued and reveled in. You need to lock in the memory of feeling creative. Try to have every cell participate in this experience. What moves you is always enough. You don't have to look for more than your heart's desire fulfilled. Right now, in this moment, what is inspiring you? Look back over your day. Can you remember anything you did, saw, said, and heard that felt creative? Close your eyes and imagine your body filled with this experience. Write it down, draw it, paint it, reflect on it, tell friends about it. The things that you long to express, you must express. The journey of self-expression must be undertaken for two different but related reasons: the world needs it and you need it. Allow the feeling of being moved to be the force that creates the drawing. We are not here to make trouble. We are here to live creatively.

Any of us who have been through career-based school systems, or perhaps grown up in families where creativity, fantasy, and daydreams were not honored and supported, may have been conditioned to bring doubt, fear, and worry to our creative processes. When we try to access the imagination, we may find a very negative shadow waiting for us. If this is your experience, remember to accept the vulnerability you feel and attempt to draw this more delicately into your work.

EXERCISE: DESIGNING FROM WITHIN

In the purest sense, "designing from within" means designing from an embodied connection with your own soul. While these words mean different things to different people, we all understand that this is not designing from the pressure to succeed or the stresses and worries over perfection. This is about designing from the place inside you where imagination, creativity, and kindness move freely. Designing from within means allowing your own deep-seated inner voices to come and go. Not too loose, not too tight, designing from within means accepting your body in the process of creating.

The aim of the exercise is to rest in its image-giving space as long as possible. For the next 20 minutes, make an agreement with yourself to put any ongoing worries or lingering conflicts aside. You can return to them later, but for now, let them go, and give yourself permission to settle into this moment.

Loosen any tight clothing and remove your glasses. Have paper and pen near by. Make sure you will not be interrupted for whatever length of time you may require.

Relaxing inwardly, let yourself settle into the sensations of your body. Take a few deep, conscious breaths letting all the messages of your body come and go. Allow any sounds you hear to arise and fade away as you begin to gently tune in to the heart of your inner designer.

Now begin to form an aspiration:

May this project be a benefit not only to myself, but to many people.
May I be as good to my client, co-workers, students, or teachers as I
    am to myself.
May this project be a positive presence.
May this project bring wellbeing and joy to all who are involved with
    its creation, fabrication, and completion.
Whatever challenges, obstacles, or hindrances that arise, may they be
    transformed positively and benefit many people.
May I be shown the way.

Now begin to imagine yourself as a designer who is fulfilled and happy. Just sink into this feeling. Really imagine yourself happy and make contact with the sensations in your mind and body. And gently, from this place, begin to imagine your project. Whatever images, thoughts or words occur, allow them to exist. Let them play and churn in your wide-open inner place of design. If you need to make a note or record an image, feel free to do so and then return to your inner studio. When you finish with an image or thought, stay tuned for whatever arises next. Make no effort to create–just rest in a generous place of acceptance.

When you sense that the energy of the exercise is finished, give thanks for all that you have received and return to the room. Take a few deep breaths and stretch before reviewing or discussing your notes and images.

Drawing on Our Own Inner Resources

Remember that we do have resources that will help us to deal with difficulties:

- We have the capacity to be aware of the present moment.
- We have the capacity to relate.
- We have the ability to make a conscious decision that supports what we truly want.
- And finally, we have the ability to take action, even when this means starting all over again.

Practicing these steps teaches us the value of awareness and relationships. Once we develop some awareness and an ability to relate everything that happens to us can become our teacher. We need to learn how to use what is difficult or we risk losing the richness of exploring who we are. We also need to remember that whatever we fail to become aware of will repeat until the lesson becomes conscious.

Hearing the Roots of the Creative Voice

There really is an inner creative voice dedicated to speaking to us in a language that helps us make design decisions. Our job is to listen without judgment and be willing to hold a space to receive this voice. We need to not overpower or squeeze it.

Carl was a very talented student. He produced remarkable drawings and models yet he usually seemed full of boiling anger. Communicating with him felt almost dangerous because the possibility that he would explode or walk away when he heard a comment he did not like was always there. For his final project, Carl had chosen to design a new inner-city community. His proposed site was an old industrial area, full of abandoned buildings, whose toxic soil had been ignored and abandoned by the city for years.

One day, as Carl was talking about his most recent drawings and models, I found myself saying, "You know, this is such a rejected site. It has always been ignored. No one has ever really cared about this place. I wonder if it will always feel rejected." I continued speaking in this way for a few minutes, talking about how unloved the place was and how toxic it had become. As we spoke, Carl's face began to change, his mouth softened and his eyes became very sad. He nodded as I spoke and agreed that the site was rejected and felt very abandoned and it was strange and even difficult to propose living there, but for reasons he did not fully understand he felt deeply drawn to the difficulty of the place. He knew this was the right place for him to start creating something new. I agreed with him and our conversation shifted to a discussion about how to approach the recovery and regeneration of this wounded part of the city.

During our conversation, it seemed for a moment that the line dividing Carl and his project had slipped away. Carl could have chosen any part of the city, but he had unconsciously been drawn to this part of the city because it reflected his own need to wrestle with a rejected part of himself. Perhaps he felt that if he could bring new growth and new hope to old and rejected places in the city, it might not seem so impossible to one day help himself.

Over the years I have seen that designers are inevitably drawn to create projects that reveal unconscious intentions. Design travels between worlds. Creative work always supports making the unconscious conscious.

The Wall

Not a shot was fired when the Berlin Wall came down. Like everyone else, I was stunned to see the images of people knocking it down with sledgehammers. After nearly 50 years the wall had come to symbolize the standoff between superpowers. As with many walls, we may never know who designed it–it was not a work of beauty but a line of war, violence, danger, and irreconcilable hatred between enemies. It was a place that separated right from wrong. The Berlin Wall showed the world where superpowers meet and how they meet. It was an ugly standoff; a world-sized symbol of harm and separation that proved no compromise was possible. It also happened to be an enormous concrete and steel wall with armed guards that divided a city. And instead of seeing the oft-threatened war of mutual destruction, we saw the wall come tumbling down in a youthful burst of liberating energy. The divided city of Berlin was made whole in an intoxicating celebration that was like some kind of ritual. I felt the almost archetypal power of a wall as symbol activated and I wondered what these images would mean for all of us who had lived with walls and separation not of our choosing.

A wall is an ordinary thing. Without walls we would not be able to make rooms. We would not be able to divide space or separate activities or have privacy. We would have no place to put our windows and doors. At one time walls were not easily built or removed; many towns and countries owed their safe existence to a strong stone wall. Successive walls measure some cities as generations of inhabitants renewed their safety by rebuilding each wall ever further from the core of the town. Today a wall is not a realistic way of defending ourselves from military attack. But we remain dependent on walls for psychological protection and emotional safety. With psychological walls come the idea of boundaries, divisions, and separation as well as the possibility of breakthroughs and openings.

As I watched the destruction of the Berlin Wall in 1989, I wondered if something inside us might also be changing, that an internal shift was now possible. Perhaps all of us who saw the images of the Berlin Wall collapsing understood that no matter what beliefs we had built, no matter how deeply held a particular attitude, or how much public effort we had made to convince ourselves and our enemies of our righteousness, our position was not permanent and could never be secure. The Berlin Wall was the greatest wall of the modern era and we all saw its fate. All walls can come down—sometimes in ways that are unexpected and unpredictable.

There are many reasons for psychological barriers, some necessary and some destructive. Emotional wall-making is often unconscious, but sometimes it is a very deliberate and carefully motivated act. When a psychological barrier is no longer needed and can come down, we enjoy the expanded freedom of movement and the sense of wholeness. We live in a larger world and gain the belief, however subtle, that other walls can and will come down. Walls carry a sense of authority that makes their collapse especially meaningful. We hear the whisper of wholeness and unification seeping through the barriers.

Berlin and much of the world rejoiced when the wall came down. The next step brought the job of re-imagining a city already filled with history that suddenly had a new important story to assimilate. The call came immediately for designs. Architects and urban designers gathered in Berlin and the work began. At immense cost, Berlin was gradually sewn back together again. Civic-scaled monuments were added to the newly unified city and restored places were configured with a conscious effort to build in a manner that honored the history of the city. The reconstruction of the wall as a zone was a broad and serious undertaking, and great economic and creative resources were applied to the task. Somehow the wall became a place that slipped into memory as well-intentioned efforts went into reclaiming space rather then holding a place for the memory of the wall.

Integrating the wall psychologically was very different from assimilating its meaning once it had been destroyed. And now, more than 15 years after the collapse of the wall, a surprising movement has begun to grow to bring back some reality of the wall. People began to miss the symbolic place. No one misses the violence and the abuse that the wall symbolized. But what happened was that people realized they needed to acknowledge the meaning of the wall. I think that people had not finished reflecting on the pain of the separation and division. The destruction of the wall had been a celebration, but perhaps the wall had been removed before there was time to grieve. Or perhaps we can't live without symbols,

especially symbols of the paradoxical and perplexing, the unfinished experience, and the unanswerable question.

We need built places that allow us to gather ourselves to reflect
on the irrational forces that effortlessly and randomly penetrate life.
And one of the new ways we can begin to understand the design of
cities is through the inclusion of places that sponsor these symbols
of both sorrow and happiness. Great cities have instinctively
understood this. A city that only remembers its great and glorious
moments is probably a city that is incomplete. We need to remember that it is more helpful to be whole than perfect, and that vision
calls for us to make places that can hold the difficult and unrecognized as well as the exceptional. We are practiced at the art of
memorializing what we want to remember, but every city might
want to ask itself, "What is it that we would rather forget?" "What
would we like never to see again?" Somehow, somewhere, we may
wish to try to make a place where this seemingly undesirable
psychic material can be safely contained and visited.

People come to Berlin today and are surprised that so little of
the wall remains. For 50 years Checkpoint Charlie was the focus of
world attention. Somehow a plaque cannot represent this
adequately. Beautiful plazas and great buildings stand where once
the wall once stood, but people seem more interested in the difficult and unfinished dark reality of the wall. What visitor to that
place doesn't have a few dark stubborn walls of separation and
isolation in their own history? Who doesn't have standoffs and
escapes? This is a call to cities to acknowledge and assimilate their
real history as a way of bringing new and shadowy place-making to
the urban world.

The last word on difficulty must go to Marie Louise von Franz,
a colleague of Carl Jung who spent many years studying alchemy,
dream, and fairy tales, and became well known for her learned
insight and full of practical advice.

Jung has said to be in a situation where there is no way out, or
to be in a conflict where there is no solution, is the classical
beginning of the process of individuation. It is meant to be a
situation without solution: the unconscious wants the hopeless

conflict in order to put ego consciousness up against the wall, so that the man has to realize that whatever he does is wrong, which ever way he decides will be wrong. This is meant to knock out the superiority of the ego, which always acts from the illusion that it has responsibility of decision. Naturally, if a man says, "Oh well, then I shall just let everything go and make no decision, but just protract and wriggle out of it," the whole thing is equally wrong, for then naturally nothing happens. But if he is ethical enough to suffer to the core of his personality, then generally...the Self manifests. In religious language you could say that the situation without issue is meant to force the man to rely on an act of God. In psychological language the situation without issue, which the anima arranges with great skill in a man's life, is meant to drive him into a condition in which he is capable of experiencing the Self. When thinking of the anima as the soul guide, we are apt to think of Beatrice leading Dante up to Paradise, but we should not forget that he experienced that only after he had gone through Hell. Normally the anima does not take a man by the hand and lead him right up to Paradise; she puts him first into a hot cauldron where he is nicely roasted for a while.

PART SIX

The Proliferation of Design

Unlike the world of long ago where nature was everywhere and design was an isolated moment, today we live in a world that is thoroughly designed and nature is more and more isolated. The toaster, the morning commute, the inside of your watch, all of this is designed. You have to travel for hours to find places where the designed world stops and the natural world begins.

The reason design matters so much is that so much of the world is designed. Everything from the location of streets to the type of trees we plant is specified if not designed and points to the influence designers. At the same time, the inability of the world we have designed to address and solve problems is evident everywhere. Commuter-based cities, sick-building syndrome, the pollution of habitats, and the rising banality of the built landscape all underscore the need for us to challenge our approach to design.

Accepting that beauty or creativity is not a priority of this society can be disappointing, but it becomes more bearable when we consider what other disciplines are also unsupported in our society. Creative and soulful design belongs to a coalition of marginalized and underappreciated fields such as education, the environment, health care, and the arts. Design is really a member of a potentially powerful alliance. It is obvious that we need hospitals and schools and places to live, but as a society we have a hard time committing to these endeavors. We are reluctant to trust the side of life that allows us to be healthy and feels good.

Designers are a necessary link in the human possibility of transformation, meaningful place-making, and generation of culture. Design contributes to our capacity to belong. Architectural imagination is one of the activities that are essential and vital to forming collective life. What these activities all have in common is their search to create what is necessary to our souls when we live in the built world. Belonging to unconscious systems, with their unconscious relationships, never makes anyone happy. I want to propose four reasons why the inclusion of the unconscious in the design of the modern built world is a worthwhile goal.

First, it is timely and necessary to make the design process more meaningful so that our modern built world more closely approximates the rich inner world experienced by every individual. Including the unconscious in architecture is not intended to make the architectural design process easier; in fact, it will probably make your work more difficult and perhaps more disturbing.

We are living in a time when advances in technology and information are rapidly re-shaping life on this planet. Yet there is also no doubt that the demands of technology increasingly conflict with its promise. I suspect this is because we are not only industrializing the world—we are also in danger of unconsciously industrializing the human beings that live here. Yet rather than fear technology or blame our appetite for discovery and invention, we need a new and modern way to remember that we are human beings. And the one discovery that makes us both modern and human is the discovery of the unconscious. Over the last 100 years, we have begun to learn how to live with the reality of the unconscious in our lives. The role of the inner studio is to give a place and time to psychological insight. This is increasingly necessary if we are to safely contain, sustain, and transform the modern world.

A day doesn't pass without some warning about what we are losing or what we have already lost from the great storehouse of the natural world. Our built world seems more and more like a reckless giant racing its own shadow. The trampled habitats, lost species, destroyed languages, and forgotten practices of vulnerable life forms are the helpless victims of an unconscious civilization. The ever-shrinking natural world haunts the proud history of modern design. Yet not that long ago we learned how to help ourselves and others from the resources that occurred naturally in this world. We were taught how to live and how to create from the uncertainty of rainfall, the way animals moved, and the way night sky changed to dawn. Today we live in the designed world and are denied the natural events and settings that once inspired and disciplined us. We are rapidly losing our capacity to understand the value of the wild and to accept the nature of things. We are in danger of forgetting that all things rise and fall naturally and that life itself is precious. We find ourselves more identified with and more dependent on the built world for our lifestyle, hopes, dreams, and inspirations. How can the built world reveal more of what we once learned from the natural world?

I think the answer rests with understanding our psyche. Our own bodies and minds are full of the psyche's wisdom and this is the starting point for the designer's transformation of the built world. The psyche is our final frontier, our greatest natural resource. It is our home, yet strangely independent and resistant to all our desires for control and power. The psyche is as magnificent, mysterious, and fragile as a vast wilderness and it is always with us. It is our most intimate geography during crucial moments of design because it is the setting for all of our creative wrestling. Psyche is the place where we synthesize our understanding and imagination and make sense of the world. And with experience, we come to know the unconscious takes the same attitude toward the ego as the ego takes toward the unconscious. How can designers bring the wisdom of the natural world to bear in their work? By tuning into their inner world during the process of design.

Tuning into a relationship with the psyche invites a new sense of meaning, beauty, and strength to enter our work. A relationship with the bright and dark dimensions of our own psyche means we learn as much from the unknowns beyond our control as we do from those experiences where we enjoy mastery. Inner events occur naturally. They are deeply programmed into our psyche because we need them to teach us inspiration and self-acceptance and help us to stay humane. Tuning into the laws of the psyche changes things from within and gives the modern soul a chance of creating physical places that make us feel at home in the built world. We will not be able to give nature its rightful place in the built world until we accept the rightful place of psyche in our lives. Provisional and everlasting, the psyche emerges as a modern and timeless place of learning.

Second, the struggle, joys, and complexity inherent in the creative process are like an invisible building material that will become transmuted into your work, giving your project the potential to express the mythic and authentically human dimensions of creativity and imagination. Working consciously with these forces will allow you to grow, and as your work becomes a built experience it will offer others a healthy place to belong.

It is difficult to make sense of the counterintuitive conditions that have become commonplace in the built world. Our beaches are unsafe for swimming in the summer, but easily pass inspection in the winter. The very chemicals that increase crop yields poison our ground water. Even though we know we are dependent on past generations for our wellbeing and future generations for our survival, we make decisions as though our life span is all that matters. The solution to the immense amount of garbage we produce has been to treat it as though it does not exist! We only believe it exists when no one wants it and we have no place to put it. What would happen if we understood these decisions as representing an accurate measure of our own wholeness? Many therapists hear very similar stories when clients explain their sorrow. We don't like pain or difficulty, but pain and difficulty exist. Given the choice of learning from difficulty or denying it, we usually deny it–this has never made anything go away or made anyone happy.

Our built world is not suffering from a lack of analysis but a lack of feeling. There is a split between what we are feeling and what we are building. In fact, symptoms of the split between our thoughts and actions, our feelings, and our deeds would send a healthy human being to a doctor. The psyche teaches us that when we ignore, undervalue, or deny aspects of ourselves, things simply go less well. Why would this not be true of our built world? If the frontier of our self-knowledge points to the need to explore unconscious content, why would we not expect the same to hold true for the way we experience the built world?

The key to understanding the world from the point of view of the psyche is to see and understand the built world symbolically. While the decisions that result in the making of the built world are highly rationalized, few are the result of truly rational thinking, which is wisdom. Rational thinking would be inclusive and unwilling to spoil aquifers and build places to live that are next to toxic landfill. Rational thinking would never spend more on weapons than health and good places to live and learn. Violence begets more and more violence, yet is steadfastly rationalized while love is forfeited and ignored because it cannot be rationalized.

Another point to consider is that if we include the unconscious in design, the process is not subject to corruption. With this approach, your work cannot become a brand or a commodity. Creative work is always under pressure to satisfy society's appetite for branded material. When your inner life is brought into your work, authenticity replaces the brand.

In the course of acquiring a more conscious imagination, there are many watershed moments, many moments of understanding, and times of insight and beauty where a transcendent experience breaks through and touches a deeper place within us. Everyone has an experience–or will one day have an experience–of place-making and belonging that almost seems like a spiritual truth. I think we need to investigate these experiences for ourselves, make them conscious, reflect on them, and draw them out.

Finally, with this approach you can develop your relationship with the psyche–what Jung called the womb of all the arts and sciences–while practicing design. The reason this point is so crucial is that it allows your creative work to be a moral undertaking without having to preach to others or be overly earnest. It also means that you can have confidence that your work, both the built and unbuilt dimensions of your design practice, can positively affect the world.

The difficulty and paradox of designing the built world as though the unconscious is real is truly great. But it is no greater than the costs of ignoring it. Since memorable design always embodies something we do not have words for, why not apply ourselves to learning about the unconscious? We are wrestling with a built world that is as lovely and wounded as we are. And this brings us full circle because the psychological meaning of beauty is wholeness. Wholeness does not promise an end to problems, it means the freedom to take on problems without being afraid of difficulty.

We need to approach design in a way that considers the reality of the whole environment the same way we look at the whole person to effect healing. This means that the conscious and unconscious aspects of the world need to be brought into the light of design. This is not a naive idea–it is a practical idea based on observing our current world. It is about the necessity for the heart and mind to wrestle with the uncontrollable energy of creation. We need to be willing to wrestle with all the energies that make our built world. This, of course, takes time to learn, time to practice, and time to implement. This is not a revolution that can happen in the space of an advertisement. We need to be willing to undertake long-term and difficult assignments. Our new understanding involves not isolating or celebrating the unconscious, but taking responsibility for it, and wrestling it down to a more consciously transformed earth.

Breaking Through

Creativity is a type of learning where the teacher and pupil are located in the same individual.
–Arthur Koestler

At the heart of design has always been the desire to make the world better. I became convinced of this through two very different experiences. First, the unshakable altruism, energy, and joy always present in the work of students when they are given the opportunity to express themselves through the act of design. Students have powerful instincts about what is missing from the world. They need a seat at the table when important decisions are being debated. Second, the seemingly infinite variety of spaces, artifacts, and places that cultures generate when they express themselves through design. The places of worship in Assisi are different from those in Kyoto, as are the teacups, houses, and streetscapes, yet there is a palpable sense of fit between place and the needs of people. This is based on a timeless sense that design is capable of fulfilling a deep and intimate call that is persistent in humanity. For centuries designers have been trying to make the built world a place where we belong, thrive, and live more happily. Living without this amounts to excluding the heart's contribution to the built world, a soul-destroying experience. Cities are great not only because of their economy and culture, but because they are where so many lives are lived.

Design is like an unlimited resource. It is unlimited because our imagination is unlimited and because its potential to do good is immeasurable. Good design is like a good deed–it travels to the ends of the earth. Design is capable of bringing to the physical world what inspiration and faith brings to our inner life. The neglected tradition in design is its inherent capacity to transform, to do good, to give light, to give spaces we feel at one with, to be a positive and joyful force in the places we live, work, and breathe. Designers can give us a physical model that reminds us what life is for.

Just as nations nominate a Poet Laureate, we need to appoint a Designer Laureate, who would serve his or her country by giving us images that express the true potential of human beings to bring what is beautiful, sustainable, and poetic to our cities, artifacts, and landscapes. A Designer Laureate would be an independent, conscious voice, constantly reminding us of the inseparability of design and living. Regardless of anyone's personal opinion about design, most would agree we are well into a situation where our survival rests on one thing: our ability to design for it.

I am imagining a conference or gathering that will reconcile the proliferation of the built world with the soulful potential of design to be a creative resource for living. Let's hope we learn to wisely create the places where we all live.

Toronto:
The City Who Is Whole

I have never been aware before how many faces there are. There are
quantities of human beings, but there are many more faces, for each
person has several.
–RAINER MARIA RILKE

Imagine if the modern city were to walk into the office of a therapist. The complaint of our city is simple: it doesn't know who it
is or how it's supposed to act. It worries about what it will become.
One day it feels whole, the next moment it feels dulled by indiffer-
ence and violence. The suffering our city feels is exhausting. It
wants beauty and charm, but doesn't know where or how to begin.
It feels drugged with infrastructure and ambition, yet it wants to
please. Seldom does a day pass without intense comparing, frustration, or crisis. What sort of personality does our city have? What
does our city project to others, and what does it know to be true in
its heart? What of the pathology and the unconscious places that
have been built and ignored? The places that are rejected are often
the only places of authenticity; the places that are embraced reflect
only what others expect us to be. Can modern cities consciously
bring into form their defining moments, their significant, often-
painful memories, their old wounds, and those hard-to-reach
places and moments that make up their true character?

What happens when urban design must include the psyche and
body of the city? Cities are as subject to addictions, delusions,
pathologies, and procrastinations as the individuals who live there.
Cities need to bring love to their difficult places. What if we were
to accept the idea that the city has conscious and unconscious

parts? What do the less understood, less visited places have to teach us?

Cities are home to citizens who dream about their neighborhoods, streets, parks, intersections, and skylines. They dream about their city dramatically collapsing, they dream about getting lost, and they dream about living in new houses. What if urban design begins to consider the city as it exists symbolically through its own spaces, neighborhoods, and places? Perhaps urban planners need an inventory of such dreams, to discover what their city is saying. What if the city could learn to become more conscious of its unconscious parts? In today's world we see cities competing like rival corporations. Every city would like to be "world class," and become a well-known brand. Cities believe they can achieve this through ambition that includes "state of the art" facilities, new attractions, and extensive advertising. While it is true that these approaches can be successful, a city may dare to take a road less traveled. She may want to do the hard work and get to know her less-visited places as a way of re-inventing herself. Psychological growth means going through the trials of self-acceptance. Our city longs for more than an extreme makeover. Our city is ready to search for what is true. Cities need both their flawed bodies and their dreamy souls in order to ripen and mature. A city needs to be the best book you will ever read.

When I hear the call to save the environment I often find myself thinking of the city. Many cities are in peril, under pressure to become brands rather then living places. They are under pressure to be copies of other cities. This is a meditation about the city where I live. It is a portrait that offers suggestions as to how cities can become psychologically richer by discovering their unique nature and building on it. Cities are more than just the places where we live and work–they define and embody what we think life is for.

Birth

Toronto was born on the north shore of Lake Ontario between two small rivers, the Humber and the Don. As with most if not all of

North American cities, native settlements and camps existed here for thousands of years before European traders arrived. The flat land surrounding the rivers and lakeshore was decent farming land and a European settlement grew into an agricultural center as well as a gateway to northern towns where the lure of fur and mineral exploitation generated a steady migration of settlers. You could say there are two kinds of towns in Ontario; mining towns and farming towns. Toronto took hold as a farming town and developed a reputation for being earnest and industrious. The Royal Winter Fair, an annual showcase of animals, farm produce, and horse-riding skills is our reminder that we are tied to the land. The early folk name for the city was Hog Town. Those less inclined to value animals came up with the name "Toronto the Good," a name that some say reflected how difficult it was to buy an alcoholic drink.

Cities as Siblings

Three hundred and fifty miles upriver was Montreal, a place that was everything Toronto was not. Montreal was charismatic, cultured, and full of grand ambition and natural good looks. It had a surplus of city riches. A mountain and a river ensured unique geography and the friction of French and English founders provided a rich and complex culture. Montreal was the obvious choice for corporate wealth and the city seemed to dance its way effortlessly into the "A" division of places in North America and the world.

Meanwhile, Toronto continued making its unremarkable decisions. The city became a scrabble of upright Victorian brick houses on a straightforward grid of tree-lined streets that formed clusters of small town-like communities, each grouped around its own main street. The differences from neighborhood to neighborhood were subtle. Every house was like a proud but modest farm house, most with wooden porches, perhaps matching bay windows, small front lawns, and back gardens. Unlike Montreal, which was built in stone, Toronto's houses featured red bricks that came from our abundant supply of clay along the Don River. A special yellow brick was used for decoration and civic buildings such as libraries. The grand projects were not the usual galleries or public spaces, but the occasional outburst of infrastructure. In Toronto beauty needed a purpose and we were mostly comfortable with projects that were practical like the R.C. Harris sewage treatment plant or the Bloor Street Viaduct. These were the great palaces in the city the way barns are great temples in the rural landscape. We remained a small town, a good place, and our charm was the self-effacing modesty of our imagination.

Growth

Then one day in 1963 everything changed. A bomb blew up a mailbox in Montreal's ruling English-speaking neighborhood of Westmount. A group that wanted Quebec to leave Canada claimed responsibility. People in Montreal were frightened and an exodus began; soon banks, small businesses, and insurance companies with thousands of their employees were headed west up Highway 401 toward Toronto.

We really weren't expecting all these Montrealers and they weren't expecting us. They were leaving a handsome, corrupt, and fun-loving cosmopolitan city with a hockey team that was unstoppable. In Toronto, drinking and dancing had been so regulated that they were nearly illegal. The city was serious about littering and illegally crossing the street. A subway system had just been built that exuded humility and restraint. The more exotic stations were named "Queen" and "King." To make matters more complex, in the wake of Montreal's trauma, the wave of immigration that had started after World War II began to grow. First came the Italians, half a million of them from southern Italy, skilled in construction trades. Then successive waves of Portuguese, Hungarians, West Indians, Chinese via Hong Kong, then East Asians, Koreans, and Greeks. Just when this surge seemed to subside, new waves of immigrants and refugees began to arrive from South America, Central America, Vietnam, Africa, and the Middle East. As is usually the case, fathers, brothers, and sons arrived and, once they had saved enough, their wives, parents, and children, brothers and sisters, aunts and uncles followed. They moved into the old downtown brick neighborhoods and started using the porches as piazzas. In place of well-kept tiny lawns, the front yards of houses now grew tomatoes and Chinese cabbage; some sported enormous Catholic statuary. Intimate tree-lined streets became international public places. Over a busy weekend front porches became new family rooms.

The shops on bland main streets started to sell saris, coffee beans, pizzas, and salami. Neighborhoods that were architecturally homogeneous began to grow a subtle exotic stubble. New colors, sounds, and smells came from the old red brick neighborhoods. The architectural fabric never changed, but each community spoke its own language and had its own radio station. Cut off from all this new energy, the traditional institutions fell asleep. But the main streets of Chinatown, Little Italy, and Little India became great. The memorable places shifted from dull provincial monuments to ethnic neighborhoods. This urban transformation was not designed, nor did politicians recognize it. The aroma of new kitchens and unfamiliar signage swept through the city like a hungry fugue. The map of the city was largely unchanged, but its way of behaving started to change. A ride on the subway became less silent. The applause at concerts became more spontaneous. While some nationalities consciously formed neighborhoods, there were plenty of places where the map of the world was redrawn. Cultures that had never communicated before shared streets, lawn-mowers, and wedding ceremonies. A public concert of an African drumming class near Little Italy led to new members of the troupe from China and Guatemala. When the Ukrainian married the Filipino, the bride's and groom's parents met to agonize over what to eat and who would wear their national costumes. We need a great public piazza where we can celebrate this during our brief summer and go tobogganing during the grey winters.

The Russians brought their down-to-earth naturopaths and excellent rye breads, the Chinese brought acupuncturists and herbalists, delicious dumplings, and noodle houses. Toronto is filled with a stunning array of healers and cooks. I shopped for dinner on three continents within the same block. Each shop morphed out of its ordinary form to greet me and then slipped back into its exotic shape, language, and smells. English was spoken briefly when my questions were answered at all. Marshall McLuhan probably got his idea for the Global Village from taking walks through the streets surrounding his office. Toronto suddenly had the whole world in its hands. The United Nations noticed and sent a plaque of recognition. Toronto grew into a vibrant city and planet at the same time. We might consider changing our name to the United Nations of Toronto.

A True Voice

You can easily find Toronto at a distance. The skyline appears dramatically as you approach, but as you draw closer, the imposing image of the city disappears. But for all its new construction, in the eyes of tourists, Toronto is most remarkable for its polite citizens and cleanliness. This is not a city of great monuments, ambitious boulevards, or dramatic parks. A more subtle force-the tolerance and energy of its many nations, gives the city its character. At its core Toronto is a healing place, not a miracle cure. We are comfortably near the top of the "B" division of cities. As a result the city has always looked to others to confirm its greatness, never realizing its own name is enough. Some say the word "Toronto" has its roots in a native word that means "meeting place."

The voice of every city is unique because it is made from the complex social and topographic DNA that arises directly out of its particular founding. A city is made from the slow and steady development of events, settings, personalities, and interactions that have filled it. A few of these moments are memorialized, but many are never recorded and they slip into the great collective urban unconscious. A city needs to recognize its unconscious as much as its needs to recognize its conscious voice. Both are needed for the creation of genuine places.

Just as millions of people were struggling to belong in Toronto, Toronto was struggling to find itself as city. The problem was a simple one. We were not confident. We did what anyone feeling inferior would do–we overcompensated.

Approaching Toronto

If you approach Toronto by car on the elevated expressway that follows the shoreline of Lake Ontario, there are several exits that will take you into the downtown, but only one can claim to be the ceremonial route into Toronto. That is University Avenue, a street that carries several of the city's key institutions–including the opera house, the courthouse, numerous insurance companies, and four large hospitals–before it finally climaxes in Queen's Park. Sitting in the center of this park like a 19th-century matron at a picnic is a great heap of Victorian stone and frumpy red-brick self-importance that is the Provincial Legislature. Wrapped around Queen's Park is the campus of the University of Toronto. When I imagine this assemblage viewed from above, the legislature resembles a pineal gland wrapped in a green brain and surrounded by the eclectic university campus–all of it sits like a radiant mind on the spine of University Avenue.

This street is so formally vast yet so creatively modest that it seems built to answer the question, "Do we have any nice clothing to wear to the theater tonight?" It passes through the edges of Chinatown, City Hall, and the Art Gallery of Ontario, but none of these places influence the life of the street. It is this feeling of emptiness and flattened monumentality that gives University Avenue its character. If the buildings of this street were faces, they would resemble the portraits found in an old men's club.

The street that officially welcomes you to Toronto is not a flamboyant ethnic boulevard, thick with pedestrians and great shops, but a dull arterial road that feels exhausted by its role of trying to link the Provincial headquarters with the place where the lake used to be. This potentially powerful vista has been disturbed and diluted by decades of landfill and other infrastructural victories until finally, like a nail in the proverbial coffin, a large office tower was erected that formally blocks the view of the lake and cuts off any chance that the life-giving waters will influence the great street. A subway line runs beneath the street and its presence helps to explain a series of elongated traffic islands that stretch down the length of the street, separating north- and southbound traffic.

These islands are stuffed with dwarf trees, fountains, flowers, war memorials, exhaust vents, and strange institutional sculptures, forming a long pile of civic decoration that reflects an unconscious narrative of the city's history, present, and future. When I first moved to Toronto, an armory sat on the site of what became the new courthouse and we watched a parade march along from the armory to the legislature. Today, there are no parades, just a strange accretion of civic and infrastructural decisions that plainly reveal the tired patriarchal persona of the city.

University Avenue is calling out to become a place. Cut off from the lake and given the characters available, I would expand the influence of the hospitals and devote the street to healing. Let's widen the sidewalks and get rid of the frozen stone monuments that divide and unnecessarily broaden the street. Let's plant long rows of echinacea, squash, corn, and ceremonial tobacco and create a healing garden. The widened sidewalks can host healing demonstrations and be filled with vendors selling massages and good food. We need to restore a thick canopy of trees that will shelter patients, workers, and citizens who use the street. We need to make a place that means something to its users and the city. While four major hospitals face the street, there are many more significant research, rehabilitation, and teaching facilities nearby, forming a remarkable healing precinct in the very heart of the city. Until this community receives a clearly themed physical presence, the warm heart of city goes unnoticed. Great dramas of birth and death play out every second in this urban precinct. Pedestrians range from the grieving to the grateful, with countless doctors, nurses, and administrators moving between facilities and appointments.

The unique life of the street deserves to be physically expressed and mirrored. We have the possibility of transforming the core of the city from a spatial statement about power to one that includes healing, feeling, and reconciliation. We could rename the street after Toronto's own Lester B. Pearson. Why name an airport after a peacemaker? We have lost our connection to the waters of life, but we need not lose the powerful link to birth, sickness, healing, old age, and death that lives at the heart of the ceremonial spine of the city.

Yonge Street

If University Avenue represents the persona of the city, Yonge Street represents it's enduring life force. Yes, it is reputed to be the longest street in the world, some say 1,200 miles in length, but for our purposes, the fact that it links several area codes is less important then what happens in its first few miles. The Yonge Street that matters most to Toronto is a small-town, honky-tonk strip that has changed less then any other part of the downtown. It is a stubborn place of bars, dollar stores, sex shops, ethnic restaurants, and used book stores that gives us a clear snapshot of what the city has on its mind when we leave it alone. The people who roam the street on summer nights looking for adventure are being secretly initiated into what urban culture has to offer. This street hosts a constant coming-out party for the younger citizens of the city. Whether you live in some dull distant suburb or have just stepped off the late bus from North Bay, Yonge Street is always waiting for you with big, open, tattooed arms. There isn't an architecturally grand or mystical moment to be found. Just people moving up and down the street in our version of an Italian passegiata. Part carnival, part urban Kundalini, part civic lesson, the role of the street is humble but important–it teaches us about the potential for collective public life in the city. My favorite nights are the weekend of Caribana, when the place floods with tourists, many from cities where walking at night is dangerous, who instantly join in the intensely sensual parade. Yes, if you are looking for clubs, good dining, or shopping, there are more popular destinations, but Yonge Street is not a destination. It is a local myth that somehow manages to always feel unaffected and slightly rural. The intense stretch from Queen to Bloor is a catwalk of a place by night and an international gallery of dollar stores by day. Short stretches of the street have been gentrified, but mostly by accidents of ambition and real estate. The street is stained and slightly desperate and allows the glands of the city to mingle and speak. It is Yonge Street that saves us from having to build a museum about the city.

Three Places We Are Not

Three brash and boldly charismatic buildings were built down-town: a huge downtown shopping center, the world's tallest freestanding structure, and a stadium for 50,000 people that features a roof that can open or close depending on the weather. The largest, the tallest, the most remarkable. They rest on the ground, but they actually seem as though they have been dropped into place from high above. We love them without affection because we built them to please and impress others. Not surprisingly, we are uneasy with their proud ambitions because of our discomfort with all things boastful or extroverted. Unconsciously, we were hoping they would help us get recognized and legitimize our city. Their lasting contribution to urban life may be that they gave the core of the city a heavy-handed mass ensuring that the downtown precinct will always have a gravity that can never be overwhelmed by the centrifugal forces of the suburbs. When the city suffers from an ugliness caused by too little thought, this can usually be seen and accepted as a kind of kitsch. When the ugliness is the result of too much thought, however, this is more difficult to redeem. Let's declare a moratorium on planning studies and let's finance an army of hungry designers to create new images of what the city could become if our goal was beauty. Every city is like an immense Self, never completed, always missing parts of its own wholeness and yet stubbornly resilient. A city gives more than it takes and this capacity for generosity that we take for granted and are so dependent on needs to be artfully supported.

So far did we drift from our true nature that when we built a new public square in the downtown on a busy shopping street, it had a strangely resistant quality. The space needs to offer instructions. We need John Candy overlooking the place the way Marcus Aurelius sits charismatically upon his horse in the Piazza del Campidoglio in Rome. Understandably, when presented with a void people actually preferred to walk around the space than through it. To stand in the emptiness that is Dundas Square, surrounded by branded advertising and news signage, is to feel like a pixel in a mildly pornographic show on high-definition TV.

Five Places About Us

The Underworld: Ravines of Don Valley

True to form, what emerged as the most wonderful parkscape in the city are the ravines that run below the level of the city streets. These invisible places hold the old soul of city, but no postcard exists to declare it. The existence of the cities soul is hidden and largely unconscious.

Many rivers and creeks define the body of the city. They begin 50 miles north of the city on what is now called the Oak Ridges Moraine. They bring the city the fresh water without which life would not be possible, yet many of these creeks and rivers have been destroyed by aggressive development and a blatant disregard for nature. Long ago the Credit, Humber, Black, Mimico, Don, and Rouge rivers carved curling troughs into the plateau, eventually giving Toronto its moist underworld. Archeologists have found numerous sites along these rivers and creeks that plainly show that Toronto was filled with communities that go back 10,000 years. But the ravines have never been incorporated into the city, let alone into the postcard images of Toronto. They abruptly end streets and stop grids, but access to them is sporadic, underdeveloped, and vague. The ravines seem to exist outside of time and space. They reveal our hidden and original nature, what we consider inferior, what the city keeps locked in its basement. Life began in these places. They are the underbelly of the city and they hold the keys to our unconscious.

Here we find all the wild, untamed, uncivilized, undesirable aspects of the city. The ravines are a refuge for the city's animals– the coyotes, foxes, and snakes. For centuries engineers sent sewers and bundled infrastructure into these sacred places. Here is where you find the homeless living in their primitive wooden huts and old Eastern European crones collecting leaves for a special herbal tincture.

On blazing hot summer days, the descent from the city's grid through a dense forest canopy gives way to a damp, cool, forest floor. The busy horizon sounds of Toronto dissolve into green light. We have reached the bottom of the city, the wet underbelly of town. Descending in space our bodies feel heavier and more at home. Descent invokes regression, solemnity, and groundedness. Signs are posted warning of the possibility of floods. We have gone down to the roots of the place. Nature quietly asserts itself and we feel at one with all life, though we have left the city far behind. Seen from below the horizon, urban life is made of fragments–the odd tower, a roofline–and coming in and out of view through the dense forest canopy, the majestic bridges that carry the city across these forgotten lands. The greatest of these, the Bloor Street Viaduct, flies like a Victorian airplane over the ravine, its reputation as a suicide platform a grim reminder of the negative power of the modern underworld. Everything is reversed now. Nature dominates and the city is occasional. The immense scale of the Don Valley is revealed. Moving along the overgrown trails reminds me of walking along streambeds in a Yucatan jungle searching for traces of the built world.

Occasionally the dank humid air of the underbelly is pierced by strange blasts of cold air as water collected from the night rains surges through storm drains forcing cool subterranean air out the overgrown drain covers. This is our accidental grotto; it's more a moment in time than a place. The potential of the ravines as sooth-ing lands remains. This is a place we need to learn from. Can places like this be built? If not how do we expand their wild and healing presence in the city? We have yet to let the fairies and earth nymphs out of their wet cradle. I think all it would take is a special flight of stairs that could link the underworld to the city. We need these places so our bodies can return to the moist world they come from. The health of the city lives here.

Lost Shoreline

The other natural feature we've lost contact with is the shoreline itself. Toronto was a port fed by the Great Lakes and the St. Lawrence River. Economics shifted the freight away, but not before Toronto filled in its shoreline first for the freighters, then the rail-ways, then the highways, and, most recently, the condominiums. The result left the city with a shoreline that seems more like an arti-ficial limb than a place where the elements mix. It is strange, not because it is cut off from the rest of the city, but because what we built at the new edge is so artificial. When we separated ourselves from the lake we became lost. We forgot where we came from and how we came to be here. When the city loses its authenticity, its soul is lost and decision making suffers.

The natural shoreline of Toronto had a name: Front Street. It is now a historical artifact 500 meters from the shoreline, but once it was on the water. Bay Street also suffered, as did most of the other major north-south arteries. We have become like a plant pulled from the ground. We suffer the disease of urban disassociation. The forces of real estate are important and need more attention than the marketing of a product. If we cannot get back to the water, perhaps we can bring water back into the city. We need to remember our watery side. We need to recall maritime weather, the portage, and the beauty of a shoreline. If the ravines speak to our loss of contact with nature, our artificial shoreline speaks to our lack of regard for the potential creativity of life. We are trying to be serious about recovering our shoreline, but we always seems to miss the point of being able to enjoy, reflect, and play at the water edge.

City Hall: Everyone Is Welcome

The old City Hall ruled Bay Street, the traditional street of wealth and power, its Victorian Gothic tower a perfect expression of patriarchy. In 1959 an architect from Finland, Vijo Revell, won an architectural competition for Toronto's new city hall. It's amazing that his project was selected by a city that until then really had shown no taste for the artful. Old and new city halls now sit side by side. The old patriarchal tower was visible from Lake Ontario. The modern city hall sits like a proud matriarch radiating welcome over her large public plaza and city. In the space between its two crescent shaped towers sits a slim pebble, the council chamber. It celebrates while exuding a slightly reserved sense of repose and hope. The ensemble spins more than sits and ensures a strong sense of invitation like the perfect northern host.

City Hall belongs to that moment when modern architecture flirted with self-expression, and so this symbol of governing is curiously more part of its creator's vocabulary than our own. That's good too because we are a city self-conscious about beauty and too introverted to like expression. City Hall is an authentically lovely place, the perfect style for Toronto. After the construction the mayor had the courage to put a large modern sculpture by Henry Moore into the square. You would have thought he had suggested poisoning the city's water supply by the opposition he encountered, but somehow he persevered. The large civic square includes a skating rink–a brilliant civic feature now copied in many towns in Ontario. On a winter's night, with skaters dancing around the rink, it's as though some secret gyroscope within the bosom of the city is in motion. The new City Hall has nothing to do with the city's architectural or cultural past and so gives Toronto a heart that anyone can claim. This is perfect for a city of newcomers. The public plaza gave us our first modern space, a place that can contain new civic identities. We need more places that can hold our global voices.

The Leslie Street Spit:
Nature Contradicted and Unintended

The way this place developed and what it has become is pure Toronto. Engineers were concerned about silt collecting in our proposed new harbor, so they carefully designed a large protective barrier out into the lake. We never built the new harbor, but we began the spit and continued to allow debris from demolished buildings and other urban excavations to be dumped here. Then a strange thing happened. Enormous numbers of migratory birds began to use the place. The spit is as flat as cardboard, but soon its top layer of bird droppings, rust, concrete, and glass was sporting a thick mat of wildflowers and grasses and soon trees took hold and the miraculous transplant was under way. Coyotes have been spotted here as they wander from the northern edge of the city to the lake.

You will always need thick-soled shoes to walk on this post-industrial earth. The place is a cross between the apocalypse and a weekend up north. It's become a great place by accident, a kind of Freudian slip of a place, and that is the way we like our great places. Unintended, so no one has to declare a vision. The archipelago reaches so far into Lake Ontario that you get to see Toronto as a distant city. There is sublime poetry here. The place attracts bird watchers and rollerbladers. After repeatedly neglecting our own nature, we accidentally created a new one, perhaps Toronto's greatest invention. Of course, there are plans to turn this strange place into something useful. But what if we saw this place as an invention. A kind of wild living laboratory, the world's first recycled park, beyond the reach of City Hall. Let's let a few ethnic restaurants set up tents for the summer under the unmanned lighthouse.

The Toronto Islands

Off the southern shore of the city lie the Toronto Islands. These flat, slender islands and lagoons form the original outer edge of the harbor. The two openings, known as the Western and Eastern Gaps, allow boat traffic to escape into Lake Ontario. The harbor is less and less of a player in the economy due to truck and rail services, but freighters that do enter the harbor are largely the very specialized Great Lakes freighters that are designed to fit through the dimensions of the locks of the St. Lawrence Seaway. The locks are most spectacular where Lake Ontario meets Lake Erie and ships must rise and fall over 300 feet to by pass Niagara Falls.

The Toronto Islands have been occupied over the last 200 years, but their character remains unchanged. Like many wonderful places in Toronto, they have never really been designed. Once thought of as a holiday place and home to cottages, the islands now comprise a small community of homes, a public park, and a small airport. Every 10 years or so there is a new fight over the islands. Should the island dwellers be removed? Should the small airport on the western edge be expanded? Should the park become more commercial? Nothing seems to change. These debates are constant and often bitter, but the Islands always defy whatever is in fashion and somehow the magic of the place slips by unharmed.

To get to the islands you must go through a miserable little terminal that is really a concrete holding pen set in a no-man's-land between condominiums. The island ferryboats look like a feminine version of the Great Lakes freighter. As the ship leaves the city edge for the islands, the joy of traveling immediately begins to transform everyone on board. The smell of the water erases the tired stink of the city and the water-born breezes arrive cooler and fresher. We are all travelers now, setting off for another world, to a new shore. The population on board is always a delightful mixture of immigrants going for picnics, cyclists, wedding parties, hardcore Island residents, and city introverts in search of silence. A nude bathing beach at Hanlon's Point rounds out the population of the typical summer traffic. This simple pleasure of a boat ride ensures this park will always be a world apart. Views back to the city have us marvel at the skyline full of the latest towers. But later, after crossing the island to the wooden boardwalk at the island's southern edge, we finally arrive at our destination: the unobstructed horizon. Water and sky frame the distance. Unfinished business stretches out forever and for a moment, the built world is gone.

Monuments That Move

The great monuments of this city are not buildings or boulevards but festivals, parades, and fairs. Seen collectively these events create instant communities of like-minded people from across the city, North America, and around the world.

A city that at one time would not allow dancing on Sundays now hosts an unabashedly spectacular Gay Pride parade. The culmination of a week of events, exhibitions, and parties, the most important aspect from an urban point of view is the route of the parade, which includes a trip down Yonge Street, the long soul of the city. The Gay Pride parade features slow-moving floats, many overflowing with barely dressed dancing men. (Lesbians hold their parade the day before.) The music is loud and remarkably, in a city where Happy Hour is illegal, everyone has totally embraced the event. Hundred of thousands of people line the parade route to dance, watch, cheer, and videotape the throbbing, subwoofer-filled extravaganza.

A few weeks later, as the summer reaches its most humid and sultry temperatures, the Caribana festival generates a parade whose rhythmic dancing erases all memories of big-city winter. This event, locally created and strongly connected to the Caribbean community, changes the soul of the city. At night the sound of drumming rings throughout the city. While not yet sited in the downtown core, this parade deserves to dance its way down the most important streets of the city before it climaxes at the water's edge.

This is just the beginning of the festival season. When the Greek community closes its street for the weekend, over a million people come to the party. The end of summer is marked by a two-week international film festival that transforms the city into a film-lover's dream. The city has a deep connection with film through long winters when the only light seems to be inside movie theaters. From Marshall McLuhan to SCTV to David Cronenberg, the city has always been a media town. Toronto's ordinary good looks have allowed the city to pose as countless foreign cities, creating a boon for the local television and film business.

For the last 75 years the Royal Winter Fair has marked the end of the growing season with a show of prize Holsteins, horses, vegetables, and animal auctions. Contestants and exhibitors come from around the world. After the Royal Winter Fair, winter begins to quiet things down. Of course most of the city is playing hockey, with some of the best games being played on outdoor rinks that depend on cold nights and volunteers who take care of the ice. Spring has returned when a day-long closing of the expressways for a bicycle sponsorship day brings another community to everyone's attention.

If I were mayor I would create a new post: Director of Parades, Festivals, and Street Fairs. The job would synchronize and plot events across the city. The key is to match events with the city's physical resources. The Royal Winter Fair could expand their tradition by marching livestock down Yonge Street. We need an official bicycle or car race that uses a course made from the expressways that surround the city, giving Toronto its modern walls. A single orbit of the city is about 25 miles.

We need a day-long festival that gathers parades from all the ethnic main streets to a great meeting on the water's edge. We need to bring back the portage and make speed skating an urban activity. These new events would accompany the already popular authors' festival, world music festival, theater festival, car shows, and Santa Claus Parade. Less demanding than the Olympics, we need only issue a calendar and a map. When we accept our nature, we honor the world that lives here and feels welcomed. No mean achievement. We continue to worry that we must do something special to become world class. But our path reveals what has made us special. We are potentially a model to the whole world of the whole world. That's our claim to being world class. That is why a modern city without the help of ancient monuments or medieval streets can seem as layered and mysterious as an astrologer's calculations.

The City and the Cemetery

Our great departed citizens, from Joyce Wieland to Jane Jacobs, from Lester Pearson to Robertson Davies are all remembered by some plaque or room to call their own, but rarely do we create public places that allow us to commune and mingle with the spirits of our ancestors. Where are the slightly over-scaled statues that energize public space? If we can't have Hercules wrestling with lions or Athena, perhaps we can have a larger then life Frank Mahovalich about to take a slap shot or Marion Hilliard holding a baby. The stories of a winning goal or a pioneering obstetrician speak to us. We need to be able to walk in places where we can talk with our ancestors and learn from their physical posture how to be in the world. Why should we allow loneliness when the souls of all of these great human beings are so near? Where can we go to find ourselves through the eyes of the city's elders? The Lester Pearson plaza, the avenue of hockey heroes or great scientists, teachers, artists, and musicians—let's use civic places to bring our ancestors out of time and into space. Of course this will cost money. Good things are expensive. We need to build the spiritual infrastructure of the city as much as we need to plan and construct highways and water treatment plants. Rarely does someone decide to see a therapist when things are going well. Mostly we need to experience a catastrophe to even think about looking at ourselves. Let's not wait. Let's change the city from within. Let's not be like other places. Let's not host the Olympics. Let's become the city ridiculed for spending some of our wealth on supporting the soul of the city.

Death and the City

Missing from the recent explosion of development in the down-town core is the construction of new cemeteries. The densification of the city has been the single greatest force of development in the last 40 years and offers us a unique opportunity to influence the city's fabric and character. But strangely, while we celebrate where all the new Torontonians are choosing to live, we ignore the fact that these same people will one day die and need to be buried. Do we bury them back in the suburbs? Those who made the decision to live, eat, make love, and raise families downtown deserve to be remembered downtown. We need to commission new urban ceme-teries to gives some soul to the financially driven housing market. Life and death is the other kind of supply and demand. A new cemetery near the under-utilized Princess Gates would give us a spiritual gate overlooking the Western Gap with a majestic view of Lake Ontario. Of course a cemetery need not be large. There are countless parking lots in the city waiting for residential develop-ment; perhaps we need to think about neighborhood places for the dead to bring depth and character to the places for the living. The developers were given their chance and have spoken. Let's not ignore the potential role of death, grief, and the rituals of burial to anchor and perpetuate the rebirth of the city.

Toronto Made Whole

An ark of a city: two of every kind and ecologically committed, we need to unearth the simple farming place we have always been. We need to take care of our animals, windmills, tree canopy, and aquifer. Toronto the Good, midwife of the Global Village.

All cities need to visit a therapist from time to time and talk about the unresolved, the unfinished, and the inexpressible. Missed opportunities abound as do unappreciated places and rejected ambitions. We are not suffering from all the bridges and buildings that fall down, but from all the ugly ones that stay up and give nothing back to the city. If cities are to continue to be relevant then we need to incorporate knowledge of the unconscious in our design work because it offers us the wisdom to withstand the centrifugal forces that otherwise threaten to tear the city apart. It is entirely practical to make the design of cities more psychological so that the places we create can become more relevant to the complex human experiences we all have.

Cities mature through hearing their genuine voices. In Toronto "visible minorities" make up nearly half the population and only slightly more then half of all her citizens call English their predominant language. When ethnicity or language fails to connect us, the soulful places of the city can effortlessly unite us. The problem is that we have never been willing to recognize the importance of such places and make their creation a priority. Cities have no choice but to mirror the collective depth, longing, desires, and confusion of their times. If we want the richness of authentic places we need to listen to the dreams, frustrations and creations of Toronto and begin to understand the city as a living symbol. Let's draw a new map of the city that proposes a route linking the great public spaces of the city. Once a year, on Thanksgiving, let's join in a city-wide procession that begins in the many different neighborhoods and winds slowly but surely towards the heart of the city. Let the entire route become a potlatch feast that brings holiness and belonging down into the streets. I imagine an annual procession, a coronation of the civic soul that brings gridlock, street food, and theater into the life of the city. Where will we gather to give thanks at the end of such a journey?

Resources

Campbell, J. *The Mythic Image*. Princeton, NJ: Princeton University Press, 1974.

Clements, R. *Analyzing Your Dreams*. 1997 (self-published).

Ellenberger, H. *The Discovery of the Unconscious*. New York: Basic Books, 1970.

Emoto M. *The Hidden Messages of Water*. Hillsboro, OR: Beyond Words Publishing, 2004.

von Franz, Marie Louise. *The Interpretation of Fairy Tales*. New York: Spring Publications, 1970.

von Franz, Marie Louise, and J. Hillman. *Jung's Typology*. New York: Spring Publications, 1971.

Gowain, S. *Creative Visualization*. New York: Bantam Books, 1979.

Halprin, M. *Imagine That!* Dubuque, IA: Wm. C. Brown Company, 1982.

Hay L. *Heal Your Body*. Carlsbad, CA: Hay House 1982.

Hollis, J. *Under Saturn's Shadow*. Toronto: Inner City Books, 1994.

Johnson, R. *Inner Work*. New York: Harper Collins, 1986.

Jung, C.G. *Dreams, Memories and Reflections*. New York: Vintage Books, 1961.

Neumann, E. *The Origins and History of Consciousness*. Princeton, NJ: Princeton University Press, 1954.

Otto, R. *The Idea of the Holy*. Oxford: Oxford University Press, 1933.

Richo, D. *How to be an Adult*. Mahwah, NJ: Paulist Press, 1991.

Sheldrake, R. *The Sense of Being Stared At*. New York: Random House, 2003.

Woodman M. *Addiction to Perfection*. Toronto: Inner City Books, 1972.